CAREERS
FOR

EXTROVERTS
& Other
Gregarious Types

VGM Careers for You Series

CAREERS

F O R

EXTROVERTS
& Other
Gregarious Types

Jan Goldberg

VGM Career Horizons
NTC/Contemporary Publishing Group

Library of Congress Cataloging-in-Publication Data

Goldberg, Jan.
    Careers for extroverts & other gregarious types / Jan Goldberg.
       p. cm. — (VGM careers for you series)
      ISBN 0-8442-2973-3 (cloth). — ISBN 0-8442-2976-8 (pbk.)
      1. Vocational guidance. 2. Extraversion. I. Title. II. Title:
Careers for extroverts and other gregarious types. III. Series.
HF5381.5.G5682   1999
331.7′02—dc21   99–34550
                                               CIP

Published by VGM Career Horizons
A division of NTC/Contemporary Publishing Group, Inc.
4255 West Touhy Avenue, Lincolnwood (Chicago), Illinois 60712-1975 U.S.A.
Copyright © 2000 by NTC/Contemporary Publishing Group, Inc.
All rights reserved. No part of this book may be reproduced, stored in a retrieval
system, or transmitted in any form or by any means, electronic, mechanical,
photocopying, recording, or otherwise, without the prior written permission of
NTC/Contemporary Publishing Group, Inc.
Printed in the United States of America
International Standard Book Number: 0-8442-2973-3 (cloth)
                                        0-8442-2976-8 (paper)
00 01 02 03 04 05 LB 18 17 16 15 14 13 12 11 10 9 8 7 6 5 4 3 2 1

This book is dedicated to the
memory of my beloved parents,
Sam and Sylvia Lefkovitz,
and the memory of a dear uncle,
Bernard Lefko.

Contents

Acknowledgments

The author gratefully acknowledges:

- The numerous professionals who graciously agreed to be profiled in this book

- My dear husband, Larry, for his inspiration and vision

- My children, Sherri, Deborah, and Bruce, for their encouragement and love

- Family and close friends—Adrienne, Marty, Mindi, Cary, Michele, Paul, Michele, Alison, Steve, Marci, Steve, Brian, Steven, Jesse, Bertha, and Aunt Helen—for their faith and support

- Diana Catlin, for her insights and input

- Betsy Lancefield, editor at VGM, for making all projects rewarding and enjoyable

CHAPTER ONE

Attention: Extroverts

Man absolutely cannot live by himself.   ERICH FROMM

In everyday language, the word *extrovert* refers to a sociable person who makes friends easily. The Swiss psychologist Carl G. Jung gave it a more technical definition by saying that extroversion meant "turning the interests and energies of the mind towards events, people and things of the outer world." In other words, extroverts are likely to be more focused on whatever is going on around them than on their own thoughts and feelings.

Are You an Extrovert?

He who lives only for himself is truly dead to others.
PUBLILIUS SYRUS

Are you the kind of person who looks outside yourself? Do you want to follow a career that allows you to interact with others? If you're not sure, take the following quiz and you'll find out!

Extrovert Quiz

1. Do you usually enjoy a good rapport with others?

2. Do you have a sincere desire to please others?

3. Do you enjoy working in groups?

4. Do you like the idea of working with others for the common good?

5. Would you rather work in a crowded office than in an isolated lab?

6. Does it bother you if you are cut off from dealing with people?

7. Do you find it easy to relate to a variety of people—even if you don't know them?

8. Do you feel rewarded when others are enriched by your actions?

9. Do you adapt easily to a flexible schedule, one that might include more than forty hours per week and nights and/or weekends?

10. Would you be able to travel if necessary?

11. Are you willing to continue to attend seminars, workshops, etc., to keep your skills sharp and perhaps improve on them?

In this book, the following careers are explored as some of the occupations that extroverts would do well to consider: careers in acting, careers in music and dance, careers in sales, careers in politics, careers in marketing and advertising, and careers in public relations and fund-raising. Though these are, by no means, the only possibilities for extroverts, they will afford you a long list of careers to consider.

A man wrapped up in himself makes a very small bundle.
BENJAMIN FRANKLIN

CHAPTER TWO

Careers in Acting

Attempt the impossible in order to improve your work.
BETTE DAVIS

T he world of acting includes a multitude of possibilities for those who like to perform. Do you enjoy being in the spotlight, providing enjoyment for others? Actors do.

Zeroing in on What Actors Do

Whether portraying someone young or old, dramatic or comedic, actors bring their characters "to life" using voices, gestures, and movements. Though acting is often viewed as a glamorous profession, the truth is that many actors are forced to put in long and irregular hours (including rehearsals and performances) with little payment in return. In addition, only a few actors achieve recognition as stars on the stage, in motion pictures, or on television. A somewhat larger number are well-known, experienced performers, who frequently are cast in supporting roles.

Most actors struggle to break into the profession and pick up parts wherever they can. As a result, many successful actors continue to accept small roles, including commercials and product endorsements. Some actors employed by theater companies teach acting courses to the public.

Qualifications and/or Training for Actors

Experienced actors recommend that those who aspire to this profession should take part in high school and college plays in order to gain experience. Large cities such as Chicago, New York, and Los Angeles have public high schools dedicated to focusing on the performing arts.

Formal dramatic training and/or acting experience is generally necessary, although some people enter the field without either. Training following high school can be obtained at dramatic arts schools in New York and Los Angeles and at colleges and universities throughout the country offering bachelor's or higher degrees in dramatic and theater arts. A master's degree in theater is considered a plus. Most people take college courses in liberal arts, theater, directing, play production, design, playwriting, speech, movement, acting, and dramatic literature. Training in singing and dancing is especially useful. Many experienced actors continue to take additional formal training to learn new skills and improve existing ones.

Desirable Traits

Desirable personal qualities for actors include talent, determination, perseverance, social skills, a good memory, a fine speaking voice, creative ability, and the versatility to portray different characters. Actors must have poise, stage presence, the ability to affect an audience, plus the ability to follow directions. In addition, physical appearance can definitely be a deciding factor in being selected for particular roles.

Actors also need stamina to withstand the heat of stage or studio lights, heavy costumes, the long, irregular hours, and the adverse weather conditions that may exist "on location."

Building a Career

The best way to start building an acting career is to pursue local opportunities and move on from there. Basic experience can be acquired through modeling, acting groups, and local and regional theater. Any or all of these may help in obtaining work in the major entertainment markets—New York or Los Angeles.

Most actors list themselves with casting agencies that help them find parts. Many also take advantage of the services offered by the unions listed at the end of this chapter. Many professional actors rely on agents or managers to find work, negotiate contracts, and plan their careers. Agents generally earn a percentage of an actor's contract.

As actors' reputations grow, they work on larger productions or in more prestigious theaters. Actors also advance to lead or specialized roles. A few actors move into acting-related jobs as drama coaches or directors of stage, television, radio, or motion picture productions. Some teach drama in colleges and universities.

The length of a performer's working life depends largely on training, skill, versatility, and perseverance. Some actors continue working throughout their lives; however, large numbers also leave the occupation after a short time because they cannot find enough work to make a living.

Extra! Extra! Read All About It!

In addition to the actors with speaking parts, "extras," who have small parts with no lines to deliver, are used throughout the industry. To become a movie extra (also known as a "background artist"), one must usually be listed with a casting agency, such as Central Casting, a no-fee agency that supplies all extras to the major movie studios in Hollywood.

Acting Strategies—Finding a Job

Armed with your college degree, basic knowledge of the acting business, and some experience, you'll need to prepare a portfolio that will highlight your qualifications, acting history, and special skills. This will take the form of a resume along with photos, or "head shots," taken by a professional photographer whom you trust to show you off to your best advantage. Attach your resume to the back of your picture with staples at the upper left and right hand corners. Once you have your portfolio ready, you can start making the rounds of casting offices, ad agencies, producers' offices, and agents. Several trade newspapers contain casting information, ads for part-time jobs, information about shows, and other pertinent data about what's going on in the industry. Among these are *Back Stage* and the weekly *Variety* in New York and Los Angeles and *Ross Reports* in New York. In Los Angeles, there's also *Daily Variety*, *Hollywood Reporter*, and *Drama-Logue*. You can even find out about casting calls and other opportunities through the Internet.

Once you drop off your resume and head shots, you certainly shouldn't just sit at home waiting for the phone to ring. Stay active by remaining in contact—it may even be a good idea to drop by the various offices and say hello. Be sure to check in by phone every week to see if any opportunities are available for you. If you are currently in a show, send prospective employers a flyer. This shows them that you are a working actor.

Audition Tips

When you get past this initial stage and actually win an audition, here are some things you should remember:

1. Be prepared.

2. Be familiar with the piece—read it beforehand and choose the parts you'd like to try out for.

3. Go for it—don't hold back.

4. Speak loudly and clearly—project to the back of the room.

5. Take chances.

6. Try not to be the one going first—if you can. Observe others so that you can pick up on what the evaluators seem to like or dislike.

7. Be enthusiastic and confident.

8. Keep auditioning—even if you don't get parts, you are getting invaluable experience that is bound to pay off at some point.

When Do You Get an Agent?

The answer: not right away. You don't need an agent to audition for everything, and there are many roles you can audition for that do not require an agent, such as theater or films. However, most commercials are cast through agencies, so you would most likely need an agent to land one.

Compensation for Actors

While waiting to be chosen for a part, it is common for acting hopefuls to take jobs as waiters, bartenders, taxi drivers, etc.— workers who are afforded a flexible schedule and some money to live on.

Minimum salaries, hours of work, and other conditions of employment are covered in collective bargaining agreements between producers of shows and unions representing workers. The Actors' Equity Association represents stage actors; the Screen Actors Guild (SAG) and the Screen Extras Guild cover actors in motion pictures, including television, commercials, and films; and the American Federation of Television and Radio Artists (AFTRA) represents television and radio performers.

According to limited information, the minimum weekly salary for actors in Broadway stage productions is $1,000. Those in small "off-Broadway" theaters receive minimums ranging from

$380 to $650 a week, depending on the seating capacity of the theater. Of course, any actor may negotiate for a salary higher than the minimum. For shows on the road, actors receive an additional amount, about $100 per day, for living expenses.

Actors usually work long hours during rehearsals. Once the show opens, they have more regular hours, working about thirty hours per week.

According to the Screen Actors Guild, motion picture and television actors with speaking parts earn a minimum daily rate of about $500, or $1,750 for a five-day week. Those without speaking parts—the extras—earn a minimum daily rate of about $100. Member actors also receive contributions to their health and pension plans and additional compensation for reruns.

Earnings from acting are low because employment is so irregular. The Screen Actors Guild also reports that the average income its members earned from acting is $1,400 a year, and 80 percent of its members earned less than $5,000 a year from acting. Therefore, many actors must supplement their incomes by holding jobs in other fields.

Some well-known actors have salary rates well above the minimums, and the salaries of the few top stars are many times the figures cited, creating a false impression that all actors are highly paid. Many actors who work more than a set number of weeks per year are covered by a union health, welfare, and pension fund, including hospitalization insurance, to which employers contribute. Under some employment conditions, Actors' Equity and AFTRA members receive paid vacations and sick leave.

Words from the Pros

Introducing Jennifer Aquino, Actor

Jennifer Aquino studied theater and dance at the University of California in Los Angeles and received a bachelor of arts degree in economics. As a member of the dance team, she was a UCLA cheerleader for three years. In addition to cheering for UCLA's football and basketball teams, she also entered national dance team competitions.

"I grew up in Cerritos, California, and received my first taste of acting at St. Linus elementary school in Norwalk, where I played the leading role of the princess in *Beyond the Horizon*," says Aquino. "Happily, I received the Performing Arts Award while attending Whitney High School.

"Following my college graduation, I got my first break playing Eolani, the wife of Dr. Jacoby in David Lynch's television series *Twin Peaks*. (This was a result of my very first audition!) Then I got an agent and joined the Screen Actors Guild. I have been performing in various theatrical productions and am a founding member of Theatre Geo, as well as an active member of Theatre West and the East West Players Network.

"My television credits include *Weird Science*, *The Paranormal Borderline*, *Fresh Prince of Bel Air*, *Santa Barbara*, and *Twin Peaks*.

"Film credits include *The Party Crashers*, *Prisoners of Love*, AFI's *it makes you wonder . . . how a girl can keep from going under*, UCLA's *Fleeting Vanities of Life*, USC's *Unexpected Love*, and NYU's *Free Love*.

"Theater credits include *People Like Me* at the Playwrights Arena; *Gila River* at Japan America Theatre and at Scottsdale Center for the Arts in Arizona; *Cabaret* and *Sophisticated Barflies* at East West Players; PAWS/LA Gala Benefit at the Pasadena Playhouse; S.T.A.G.E. Benefit at the Luckman Theatre; *The Really Early Dinner Theatre for Kids* at The Hollywood Playhouse; *Boys' Life*, *Hold Me!*, *Scruples*, and *Watermelon Boats* at Theatre West; *Mistletoe Mews* at Theatre Geo; and *Is Nudity Required?* at Playhouse of the Foothills.

"I remember performing at family gatherings ever since I was a small child," says Aquino. "I always enjoyed being in the spotlight. To me, acting is like a child's game of pretend, something I always enjoyed. I see it as a career where you can earn a lot of money while having a lot of fun. At the same time you are entertaining people, affecting them, making them think, helping them to feel certain emotions, educating them, and helping them escape from their current lives.

"Most actors who are starting out hold some kind of side job, day job, or part-time job. For me, it was a career in the health care industry working for Kaiser Foundation Health Plan. I then became a Health Care Consultant for one of the Big Six accounting firms, Deloitte & Touche LLP. I was such a good employee that my managers were flexible and let me go out on auditions.

"After a few years, I realized that I was working too many hours, (seventy to eighty per week), and I finally had to make a decision to quit my day job and focus 100 percent of my time toward acting. After booking a few jobs, including a national commercial, I was able to do so. It was a big risk, but one I felt necessary to take. I remember what my acting coach would say— 'Part-time work gets part-time results.' The more I put into acting, the more I got out of it.

"Don't be fooled," stresses Aquino. "Acting is a lot of hard work! I am at it seven days a week, mornings, afternoons, evenings, weekends (forty to sixty hours per week). And if I'm not working on the creative side of acting (which is doing my homework for a job that I booked or for an audition), I am working on the business side of acting—talking to agents or managers; networking; sending my head shots to casting directors, producers, directors, writers; attending seminars; meeting people. I also try to keep my stress level down and take care of myself by getting enough sleep, exercising, eating healthy foods, and having some relaxation time. And I have been fortunate—the sets I've worked on have all been positive experiences for me.

"What I like most about my work is that I can say that I am making a living doing what I absolutely love to do, and that I am pursuing my passion in life. Not too many people in this world can say that. What I like least about my work is that there is a lot of politics in it. It's not always the best actor who gets the job. Sometimes it's a certain look, or your credits, or who you know, or a combination of factors that determines who gets the job. In other words, there are a lot of things that are out of your control. That's just part of the business and you have to accept it.

"I would advise anyone who is considering acting as a career to pursue your dreams and be persistent—but only if it's something you absolutely love to do, and there's nothing else in the world you would rather do. Pursue the creative as well as the business side of acting. Don't let anyone stop you from doing what you want to do. And always keep up your craft by continuing your training."

Introducing Gonzo Schexnayder, Actor

Gonzo Schexnayder earned a bachelor's degree in journalism and advertising at Louisiana State University in Baton Rouge. He attended various acting classes at LSU and Monterey Peninsula College in Monterey, California. He also attended Chicago's Second City Training Center for over a year and The Actors Center following that. He is a SAG and AFTRA member.

"I had always wanted to do stand-up comedy but didn't pursue it until graduating from college, when I began working with an improvisational comedy group," explains Schexnayder. "Four months later, the military sent me to Monterey, California, for language training. While there, I did my first staged reading and my first show. I'd never felt such elation as when I performed. Nothing in my life had given me the sheer thrill and rush that I experienced by creating a character and maintaining that throughout a given period of time. Nothing else mattered but that moment on stage, my other actors, and the scene we were performing.

"After completing the language program in November of 1990, I returned to Baton Rouge. There I began the long process of introspection about my career choices and what I wanted to do. I began to audition locally and started reading and studying acting. I still had not made the jump to being an actor. I was merely investigating the possibility.

"One night, while watching an interview with John Goodman, I realized how important acting had become to me. I knew that it possibly meant a life of macaroni and cheese, but I knew that up until that moment, nothing had made me as happy or as motivated. While I believe I had the skills and the drive to make it in advertising (or whatever career I chose), I decided that acting was my only logical choice.

"Whether it's rehearsing a show, performing improvisation in front of an audience, or even auditioning for a commercial, it's fun. If you can separate the sense of rejection most actors feel from not getting a part, auditioning for anything becomes your job. Rehearsing becomes your life. Just as a carpenter's job is building a house, as an actor, I look at my job as building my performance. The final product is there for me to look at and admire (if executed well), but the path to that product is the thrill.

"Unfortunately, I'm not at a point in my career where I'm making enough money to quit my day job. I'm close, but not close enough. I still feel the need to have some sense of financial stability or I lapse into thinking about money. It's all about balance and deciding what's really important. Sure, I'd love to have an apartment with central air and a balcony. I'd love to have a car that is still under warranty. But I know that by putting my efforts and money into my acting career, those other things don't matter. What matters is how it makes me feel. Cars and apartments don't give me the satisfaction that being an actor does.

"How many hours and how busy I am depends on what I'm doing. Over the last year I've worked with five other actors to open our own theater, Broad Shoulders Theatre, and have found my time constrained. On top of that I have been pursuing (with some success) a voice-over/on-camera career in addition to working a full-time job. Yesterday I finished six days of shooting on a graduate thesis film and last weekend we opened our first show (TheatreSports/Chicago, Improvisational Comedy) at our new theater. We have another opening (which I'm not performing in) tonight and expect to open four more shows in the next three months. I've also taken a year of guitar classes and maintained my presence in acting/on-camera classes and workshops. I'm always busy and continually looking for the next chance to market myself and increase my salability as an actor (train, study, perform, work).

"I love the process of acting and sometimes just the fast-paced, eclectic nature of the business. There is always something new to learn and something new to try. The sheer excitement of performing live is amazing and the personal satisfaction of getting an audience to laugh or cry simply by your words and actions is very gratifying.

"The sad fact is that there are people who enjoy taking advantage of an actor's desire to perform. As one of the only professions where there is an abundance of people willing to work for nothing, producers, casting directors, agents, and managers who only care about the money sometimes abuse actors for personal gain. Being an astute actor helps prevent much of this, but one must always be on the lookout.

"I would advise others who are interested in this career to stay and work where you are. Perfect your craft. Then move when you *have* to. You will know when it's time. And above all, trust your instincts."

Introducing Jack Stauffer, Actor

Jack Stauffer, a graduate of Northwestern University, has been a working actor since 1968. He created the role of Chuck Tyler in the popular television daytime drama, *All My Children*, and remained in that role for three and a half years—a total of 386 shows. Other regular television appearances include *Battlestar Galactica* and *The Young and the Restless*. Episodic television appearances include *Lois and Clark, Viper, Designing Women, Quantum Leap, Perfect Strangers, Growing Pains, Knots Landing,* and *Dynasty.* In all, he has appeared in forty prime-time television shows and numerous movies-of-the-week and mini series. He was also co-star in the movie, *Chattanooga Choo Choo.* In theater, he had parts in *My Fair Lady* and *Oliver* at the Grove Theatre in San Bernadino County. Other play productions include *The Music Man, Annie Get Your Gun, Fiorello, Can Can, The Music Man, Mister Roberts,* and *Guys and Dolls.* His list of achievements also includes parts in more than two hundred commercials.

"I started as a child actor but really didn't become a professional until I graduated from college in 1968," says Stauffer. "I simply sold my car, moved to New York, and hit the pavement!

"Since I grew up in the industry, I was well acquainted with how things work," he explains. "My mother worked for Warner Brothers and was W. C. Fields' radio producer. My father produced the *March of Time* for radio during World War II. He then founded his own advertising agency and was responsible for many early television series in the days when the ad agencies had tremendous creative input into a television show. Many notable celebrities used to spend time in our living room. As long as I can remember, I have always wanted to be a performer. It has been my burning desire despite my parents' best efforts to dissuade me from the vagaries of the industry. They would have been happy for me to pursue a more stable and lucrative career.

"Unless you are on a series or are a celebrity, you are constantly battling the belief that you will probably never work again. Thus, your workday consists of looking everywhere and calling anyone who might give you a job. Once you have done all you can do, you inevitably wait for the phone to ring. The vast majority of the time, it doesn't. So, most actors have other jobs—temporary work, or selling, or in my case, teaching tennis—anything to make enough money to pay the bills so you can pursue your craft. When you are finally hired for a day or a week or a month or whatever it might be, every moment in your day suddenly has purpose. You get to do what you were meant to do, even if it is only for a short time or if the part is minuscule. You are on top of the world. Then it is over, and it is back to square one.

"The best thing about your work is the work itself. An actor lives by his emotions and his ability to convey them to an audience. A good actor makes it look easy even though it is very hard. This partially explains why so many actors are willing to work for free. It is the work that fulfills them. Of course, if you get paid, it is much better. The recognition factor is important also. That is why so many actors return to the stage. The gratification is immediate. Any actor who says the applause means nothing to him is probably lying.

"The worst thing about the industry is that absolute lack of tenure. You are only as good as your next job. Your history, experience, etc., don't mean much. This is because there is no studio system anymore. With no continuity, it is difficult to slowly work your way up the ladder of success. The easiest way to get hired today is to have the executive producer of a hit show as your brother-in-law.

"The question I am asked more than any other is how to get into this industry, and the answer is easy. If you have an absolute, undying, uncontrollable passion to do this—and I mean you will die if you don't—then by all means give it everything you've got. But if you are the slightest bit timid or unsure, choose another career. This is a business based on rejection, and it can destroy you. If you sell cars and somebody doesn't buy one, they simply don't want that car. As an actor, when you are turned down, they don't want *you*. It's difficult *not* to take it personally. You have to be very strong to keep at it."

Introducing Joseph Bowman, Actor

Joseph Bowman is an actor in the Los Angeles area who considers himself at the beginning stage of his career. A high school graduate, he has some college, vocational, and military training in his background and also participated in the Vanguard Theatre Ensemble Training for four years.

"I was in the Marine Corps for six years and attained the rank of sergeant via meritorious promotion," says Bowman. "I thoroughly loved the United States military. It tended to reward a person who acted as if he enjoyed this kind of life, and I was such a person. It seems that I have always been able to act appropriately in any given situation. Older people usually find me charming. Younger people usually find me cool. I love to be the chameleon.

"Five years ago, a friend was attending a model/talent showcase that piqued my interest. I ended up doing it, and he didn't. Even though it was a fiasco, it had revived in me my love of performing.

"At my present level, I do a lot of background work. My military experience gets me a lot of work in productions that have a need for people who have 'been there' to add a flavor that normal actors don't always possess. Much of this work involves firing military weapons (blanks) and the knowledge of the safety concerns therein.

"There are not many typical days in acting because every production is very different. It is like working for a different company in a different capacity every day. I may be asked to simply put on a costume and chat (mime) with another actor for eight hours one day. Another day, I might be asked to put on the full battle dress uniform of a branch of the military and fire an M-16 at a monster that isn't there! It varies widely, and that is why I love it.

"The hours and working conditions also vary greatly. Typically, jobs consist of ten-hour days with pleasant working conditions. Sometimes a 'shoot' can be as quick as three hours, and sometimes it takes thirteen! It all depends on what the director is looking for and when he or she sees it.

"I enjoy being involved in the artistic side of life. I love the people who populate the arts. They are intelligent, funny, and varied. Nine to five has never been my style. I languish and fade under fluorescent light . . . ahhh, but shine a spotlight my way and watch me grow ten feet tall and bulletproof!

"I most enjoy the variety and the opportunity to become a character. I have worked my share of day jobs, and I hated the monotony of them. Fame is not my goal. Riches are not my goal. I simply want to do what I love and get paid for it. That is my dream.

"The only thing I don't like about acting is that there is a lot of classism. If you are on a 'shoot' as a background actor, many do not afford you the level of treatment that featured or lead actors enjoy. It is simply a fact of life. Most actors at a high level do not act snobbish to the lowest-rung actors, but many of the production people do.

"I would advise those interested in this field to study the craft and art of acting as if your life depended upon it. Enjoy life and experience it to the fullest, because good artists bring all their life experiences to their art. And don't let anyone tell you that you are a fool for following your dream. In your later years, would you rather look back and say, 'I wish I had at least tried' or 'I gave it my best shot, and had fun along the way?'"

Introducing Joe Hansard, Actor and Stand-Up Comedian

Auditioning for a television commercial at the age of five was enough for Joe Hansard to become hooked, and he currently works as an actor and a stand-up comedian in New York City. He attended trade school at the Broadcasting Institute of Maryland and has also been an actor in residence at the International Film & Television Workshops. Other training includes Stand-Up New York ('comedian school') and the Mike Fenton Scene Study Workshop for Film. He has performed his comedy routine at several comedy clubs in New York, and his favorite acting credit is the part of Jimmy Lee Shields in the pilot episode of NBC's *Homicide*.

"I've always had a fascination for the motion picture industry," Hansard says. "I enjoy the camaraderie and collaboration that comes with a film or television project, as well as the challenges. I liken it to being in a football game, where you are given the ball and you run with it. As an actor, I try to expand on the ideas given me by bringing my own uniqueness to a role.

"Since there is nothing better than working with folks who truly love their work and get excited about what they do, I like surrounding myself with creative, enthusiastic, and energetic people. As a stand-up comedian, nothing is more exhilarating than laughter and applause. It is sweeter than any candy, and it doesn't rot my teeth!

"I owe everything to my mom and dad. I performed at talent showcases in elementary school and was into magic tricks in my preteens. After high school, I didn't know what I wanted to do with my life, and mom came to the rescue again by suggesting a trade school for broadcasting. I was about nineteen or twenty when I landed my first paying gig as a DJ for an AM radio station in the college town of Shippensburg, Pennsylvania.

"I got my SAG card when director Christopher Leitch cast me in a principal role in the feature film *The Hitter,* starring Ron O'Neal and Adolph Caesar, who was an Oscar winner for *A Soldier's Story.*

"I moved to Los Angeles in the early 1980s and had an absolutely horrible experience there. I couldn't get work, had my car repossessed, went bankrupt, and was in poor shape emotionally. It was the darkest time of my life, and there seemed to be no light at the end of the tunnel. But I finally got my act together and moved back east, and that's when Barry Levinson cast me in the pilot episode of *Homicide* on NBC. The 'Gone for Goode' episode in which I appear aired after the Superbowl in 1993 and was the highest-rated *Homicide* episode ever.

"I decided to pursue stand-up comedy as a means to network and get myself 'out there.' So far I have performed at Stand-Up New York, the Comedy Store, and the Fun Factory.

"The bulk of my typical day is actually spent looking for work. I track casting leads wherever I can find them, either through personal contacts with industry professionals I've been associated with over the years, on the Internet, or just via the good old grapevine. This is a crazy business. Sometimes it's busy and full beyond belief and there's barely time to catch my breath. At other times, weeks and even months go by with nary a job in sight.

"If I'm working on a film or television show, the days are very long—between ten and fourteen hours a day. There is either a real camaraderie that forms on a set or a real paranoia, depending on any number of circumstances and variables in or out of your control that are inherent to the industry. In most cases, it is quite enjoyable, as cast and crew are very professional, and you, more often than not, will get kudos when the director or producer likes the work you are doing. I've found that the entire production and creative team literally evolves into a family.

"I like to work. I love meeting and working with creative, talented actors and directors. I love the business and wouldn't trade it for anything. But the thing I like least is not having any work, having to sit idle. In any case, I see an acting coach once a week and take classes to stay tuned up.

"I would tell others that the most important thing is to love your work. Know that there is much competition and some lean times, but always remember to enjoy what you do and have fun doing it!"

For More Information

Information about opportunities in regional theaters may be obtained from:

Theatre Communications Group, Inc.
355 Lexington Avenue
New York, NY 10017

A directory of theatrical programs may be purchased from:

National Association of Schools of Theatre
11250 Roger Bacon Drive, Suite 21
Reston, VA 22090

Additional information may be secured from the following associations:

Actors Equity Association
165 West Forty-sixth Street
New York, NY 10036

Alliance of Canadian Cinema
Television and Radio Artists
2239 Yonge Street
Toronto, Ontario M5S2B5
CANADA

Alliance of Resident Theaters/New York
325 Spring Street
New York, NY 10013

American Federation of Television and Radio Artists (AFTRA)
260 Madison Avenue
New York, NY 10016

American Film Institute
P.O. Box 27999
2021 North Western Avenue
Los Angeles, CA 90027

American Guild of Variety Artists (AVA)
184 Fifth Avenue
New York, NY 10019

American Theater Association (ATA)
1010 Wisconsin Avenue NW
Washington, DC 20007

American Theatre Works, Inc.
Theatre Directories
P.O. Box 519
Dorset, VT 05251

Canadian Actors Equity Association
260 Richmond Street East
Toronto, Ontario M5A1P4
CANADA

National Arts Jobbank
141 East Palace Avenue
Santa Fe, NM 87501

National Association of Schools of Theatre
11250 Roger Bacon Drive, Suite 21
Reston, VA 22090

Screen Actors Guild (SAG)
5757 Wilshire Boulevard
Los Angeles, CA 90036

CHAPTER THREE

Careers in Music and Dance

Music is edifying, for from time to time it sets the soul in operation. JOHN CAGE

A rthur Rubinstein learned the names of the piano keys by the time he was two years old. Ray Charles began to play the piano at age three. Yehudi Menuhin performed solos with the San Francisco Symphony Orchestra at the age of seven. Buddy Holly won $5.00 singing "Down the River of Memories" at a talent show at five. Gladys Knight won $2,000 singing on the Ted Mack Amateur Hour at age seven. Marvin Hamlisch was accepted at the Julliard School of Music at age seven. All of these musical geniuses got their starts very early as those who choose careers in music and dance often do.

About 256,000 musicians perform in the United States. Included in this number are those who play in any one of thirty-nine regional, ninety metropolitan, or thirty major symphony orchestras. (Large orchestras employ from eighty-five to more than a hundred musicians, while smaller ones employ sixty to seventy-five players.) Also counted are those who perform with small orchestras, symphony orchestras, pop and jazz groups, as well as those who broadcast or record.

Zeroing in on What Musicians Do

Instrumental musicians may play a variety of musical instruments in an orchestra, popular band, marching band, military band, concert band, symphony, dance band, rock group, or jazz group and may specialize in string, brass, woodwind, or percussion instruments or electronic synthesizers. A large percentage of musicians are proficient in playing several related instruments, such as the flute and clarinet, which increases their employment opportunities. Some who are very talented have the option to perform as soloists.

Rehearsing and performing take up much of the musicians' time and energy. In addition, musicians, especially those without agents, may need to perform a number of other routine tasks, such as making reservations, keeping track of auditions and/or recordings, arranging for sound effects amplifiers and other equipment to enhance performances, designing lighting or costuming, doing makeup, handling bookkeeping, and setting up advertising, concerts, tickets, programs, and contracts. Musicians also need to plan the sequence of the numbers to be performed and/or arrange their music according to the conductor's instructions before performances.

Musicians must also keep their instruments clean, polished, tuned, and in proper working order. In addition, they are expected to attend meetings with agents, employers, and conductors or directors to discuss contracts, engagements, and any other business activities.

The Range of Opportunities for Musicians

Performing musicians encompass a wide variety of careers. Here are just a few of the possibilities for musicians and others who love music but may not play an instrument.

Session Musician

The session musician is the one responsible for playing background music in a studio while a recording artist is singing. The session musician may also be called a freelance musician, a back-up musician, a session player, or a studio musician. Session musicians are used for all kinds of recordings—Broadway musicals, operas, rock and folk songs, and pop tunes.

Versatility is the most important ingredient for these professionals—the more instruments the musician has mastered, the greater the number of musical styles he or she can offer and, therefore, the more possibilities for musical assignments. Session musicians often are listed through contractors who call upon them when the need arises. Other possibilities exist through direct requests made by the artists themselves, the group members, or the management team.

The ability to sight-read is important for all musicians but it is particularly critical for session musicians. Rehearsal time is usually very limited and costs make it too expensive to have to do retakes.

Section Member

Section members are the individuals who play instruments in an orchestra. They must be talented at playing their instruments and able to learn the music on their own. Rehearsals are strictly designed for putting all of the instruments and individuals together and for establishing cues such as phrasing and correct breathing. It is expected that all musicians practice sufficiently on their own before rehearsals.

Concertmaster

Those chosen to be concertmasters have the important responsibility of leading the string sections of the orchestras during both rehearsals and concerts. In addition, these individuals are responsible for tuning the rest of the orchestra. This is the "music" you hear for about fifteen to twenty seconds before the musicians begin to play their first piece. Concertmasters must possess leadership abilities and be very knowledgeable of both the music and all the instruments. They answer directly to the conductor.

Floor Show Band Member

Musicians who belong to bands that perform floor shows appear in hotels, nightclubs, cruise ships, bars, concert arenas, and cafes. Usually the bands do two shows per night with a particular number of sets in each show. Additionally, they may be required to play one or two dance sets during the course of the engagement. The audience is seated during the shows and gets up to dance during the dance sets. Shows may include costumes, dialogue, singing, jokes, skits, unusual sound effects, and anything else the band decides to include. Floor show bands may be contracted to appear in one place for one night or several weeks at a time. As expected, a lot of traveling is involved for those who take up this career.

Announcer/Disc Jockey

Announcers play an important role in keeping listeners tuned into a radio or television station. They are the ones who must read messages, commercials, and scripts in an entertaining, interesting, and/or enlightening way. They are also responsible for introducing station breaks, and they may interview guests and sell commercial time to advertisers. Sometimes they are called disc jockeys, but actually disc jockeys are the announcers who oversee musical programming at radio stations and during parties, dances, and other special occasions.

Disc jockeys may also interview guests, make public service announcements, announce the time, do the weather forecast, or even report the news. They must be very knowledgeable about music in general and all aspects of their specialties, specifically the music and the groups who play and/or sing that kind of music. Their programs may feature general music, rock, pop, country and western, or any specific musical period or style, such as tunes from the 1950s or 1960s.

Since radio programs are usually performed live, disc jockeys must be quick thinking and personable. Most often they do not have a written script to simply read. They also must be able to perform well under stress and in situations where things do not go as planned. Thus, the best disc jockeys possess pleasant, soothing voices and good wit and are able to keep listeners fully entertained.

It takes considerable skills to work the radio controls, read reports, watch the clock, select music, talk with someone, and be entertaining to the audience—all at the same time.

Conductor and Choral Director

The music conductor is the director for all of the performers in a musical presentation, whether it be singing or instrumental. Though there are many types of conductors—symphony, choral groups, dance bands, opera, marching bands, and ballet—in all cases the music conductor is the one in charge of interpreting the music.

Conductors audition and select musicians, choose the music to accommodate the talents and abilities of the musicians, and direct rehearsals and performances, applying conducting techniques to achieve desired musical effects such as harmony, rhythm, tempo, and shading.

Orchestral conductors lead instrumental music groups, such as orchestras, dance bands, and various popular ensembles. Choral directors are in charge of choirs and glee clubs, sometimes working with a band or orchestra conductor.

Qualifications and Training for Musicians

Many people who become professional musicians begin studying an instrument at an early age. They may gain valuable experience playing in a school or community band or orchestra or with a group of friends. Singers usually start training when their voices mature. Participation in school musicals or in a choir often provides good early training and experience.

Musicians need extensive and prolonged training to acquire the necessary skills, knowledge, and ability to interpret music. This training may be obtained through private study with an accomplished musician, in a college or university music program, in a music conservatory, or through practice with a group. For study in an institution, an audition frequently is necessary. Formal courses include musical theory, music interpretation, composition, conducting, and instrumental and voice instruction. Composers, conductors, and arrangers need advanced training in these subjects as well.

Many colleges, universities, and music conservatories grant bachelor's or higher degrees in music. Many also grant degrees in music education to qualify graduates for a state certificate to teach music in an elementary or secondary school.

Those who perform popular music must have an understanding of, and feeling for, the style of music that interests them, but classical training can expand their employment opportunities as well as their musical abilities.

Although voice training is an asset for singers of popular music, many with untrained voices have successful careers. As a rule, musicians take lessons with private teachers when young and seize every opportunity to make amateur or professional appearances.

Desirable Personal Traits

Young people who are considering careers in music should have musical talent, versatility, creative ability, poise, and the confidence and stage presence to face large audiences. Since quality performance requires constant study and practice, self-discipline is vital.

Moreover, musicians who play concert and nightclub engagements must have physical stamina because frequent travel and night performances are required. They must also be prepared to face the anxiety of intermittent employment and rejections when auditioning for work.

Compensation for Musicians

Earnings for musicians often depend on a performer's professional reputation, place of employment, and the number of hours worked. The most successful musicians can earn far more than the minimum salaries indicated below.

According to the American Federation of Musicians, minimum salaries in major orchestras range from about $1,000 to $1,200 per week during the performance season. Each orchestra works out a separate contract with its members. The season of these top orchestras ranges from forty-eight to fifty-two weeks, with most being fifty-two weeks, or year-round. In regional orchestras, the minimum salaries are between $400 and $700 per week, and the seasons last twenty-five to thirty-eight weeks, with an average of thirty weeks. Some now work a fifty-two-week season. Community orchestras, however, have more limited levels of funding and offer salaries that are much lower for seasons of shorter duration.

Musicians employed in motion picture or television recording and those employed by recording companies are paid a minimum ranging from about $200 to $260 a week, depending on the size of the ensemble.

Musicians employed by some symphony orchestras work under master wage agreements, which guarantee a season's work up to fifty-two weeks. Many other musicians may face relatively long periods of unemployment between jobs. Even when employed, however, many work part-time. Thus, their earnings generally are lower than those in many other occupations. Moreover, since they may not work steadily for one employer, some performers cannot qualify for unemployment compensation, and few have either sick leave or vacations with pay. For these reasons, many musicians give private lessons or take jobs unrelated to music to supplement their earnings as performers.

Many musicians belong to a local of the American Federation of Musicians. Professional singers usually belong to a branch of the Associated Actors and Artists of America.

Zeroing in on What Dancers Do

Ever since ancient times, dancers have used their bodies to express ideas, stories, rhythm, and sound. In addition to being an art form for its own sake, dance also complements opera, musical comedy, television, movies, music videos, and commercials. Therefore, many dancers sing and act as well as dance.

Dancers most often perform as a group, although a few top artists dance solo. Many dancers combine stage work with teaching or choreographing.

The Range of Opportunities for Dancers

Choreographer

Choreographers create original dances. They may also create new interpretations of traditional dances, such as the *Nutcracker* ballet, since few dances are written down. Choreographers instruct performers at rehearsals to achieve the desired effect. They also audition performers.

Ballet Dancer

Ballet dancing requires a lot of training—in fact, more than any other kind of dancing. Ballet dancers are performers who express a theme or story.

Modern Dancer

Modern dancers use bodily movements and facial expressions to express ideas and moods. Jazz is an example of a modern dance.

Tap Dancer

Tap dancers use tap shoes to keep in time with all kinds of music. The shoes allow them to tap out various dance rhythms.

The Life of a Dancer

Dancing is strenuous. Rehearsals require very long hours and usually take place daily, including weekends and holidays. For shows on the road, weekend travel is often necessary. Rehearsals and practice are generally scheduled during the day. Since most performances take place in the evening, dancers must usually work late hours.

Due to the physical demands, most dancers stop performing by their late thirties, but they sometimes continue to work in the dance field as choreographers, dance teachers and coaches, or artistic directors. Some celebrated dancers, however, continue performing beyond the age of fifty.

Dancers work in a variety of settings, including eating and drinking establishments, theatrical and television productions, dance studios and schools, dance companies and bands, and amusement parks.

In addition, there are many dance instructors in secondary schools, colleges and universities, and private studios. Many teachers also perform from time to time.

New York City is the home of many of the major dance companies. Other cities with full-time professional dance companies include Atlanta, Boston, Chicago, Cincinnati, Cleveland, Columbus, Dallas, Houston, Miami, Milwaukee, Philadelphia, Pittsburgh, Salt Lake City, San Francisco, Seattle, and Washington, D.C.

Qualifications and Training for Dancers

Training for dancers varies according to the type of dance. Early ballet training for women usually begins at five to eight years of age and is often given by private teachers and independent ballet schools. Serious training traditionally begins between the ages of ten and twelve. Men often begin their training between the ages of ten and fifteen.

Students who demonstrate potential in the early teens receive more intensive and advanced professional training at regional ballet schools or schools conducted under the auspices of the major ballet companies.

Leading dance school companies often have summer training programs from which they select candidates for admission to their regular full-time training program. Most dancers have their professional auditions by age seventeen or eighteen; however, training and practice never end. Professional ballet dancers have one- to one-and-one-half-hour lessons every day and spend many additional hours practicing and rehearsing.

Early and intensive training also is important for the modern dancer, but modern dance generally does not require as many years of training as ballet.

Because of the strenuous and time-consuming training required, a dancer's formal academic instruction may be minimal. However, a broad, general education including music, literature, history, and the visual arts is helpful in the interpretation of dramatic episodes, ideas, and feelings.

Many colleges and universities offer bachelor's or higher degrees in dance. This might be through the departments of music, physical education, fine arts, or theater. Most programs concentrate on modern dance but also offer courses in ballet and classical techniques, dance composition, dance history, dance criticism, and movement analysis.

A college education is not essential to obtaining employment as a professional dancer. In fact, ballet dancers who postpone their first audition until graduation may compete at a disadvantage with younger dancers. On the other hand, a college degree can help the dancer who retires at an early age, as often happens, and wishes to enter another field of work.

Completion of a college program in dance and education is essential to qualify for employment as a college, elementary, or high school dance teacher. Colleges, as well as conservatories, generally require graduate degrees, but performance experience often may be substituted. However, a college background is not necessary for teaching dance privately or choreographing professionally. Studio schools usually require teachers to have experience as performers.

Compensation for Dancers

The earnings for many professional dancers is governed by union contracts. Dancers in major opera ballet, classical ballet, and modern dance corps belong to the American Guild of Musical Artists, Inc., AFL-CIO. Those on live or videotaped television belong to the American Federation of Television and Radio Artists. Those who perform in films and on television belong to the Screen Actors Guild or the Screen Extras Guild. Those in musical comedies are members of the Actors' Equity Association. The unions and producers sign basic agreements specifying minimum salary rates, hours of work, benefits, and other conditions of employment. However, the contract each dancer signs with the producer of the show may be more favorable than the basic agreement.

The minimum weekly salary for dancers in ballet and moder productions is about $610. According to the American Guil' Musical Artists, new first-year dancers being paid for singl' formances under a union agreement earn about $475 p' and $70 per rehearsal hour. Dancers on tour receive tional allowance for room and board. The minim mance rate for dancers in theatrical motion pict $100 per day of filming. The normal work week including rehearsals and matinee and evening performances, but it may be longer. Extra compensation is paid for additional hours worked.

Earnings from dancing are generally low because dancers' employment is irregular. Like actors and musicians, they often must supplement their income by taking temporary jobs unrelated to dancing.

Dancers covered by union contracts are entitled to some paid sick leave, paid vacations, and various health and pension benefits, including extended sick pay and childbirth provisions. Employers contribute toward these benefits. Most other dancers do not receive any benefits.

Earnings of choreographers vary greatly. Earnings from fees and performance royalties range from about $970 a week in small professional theaters to over $30,000 for an eight- to ten-week rehearsal period for a Broadway production. In high-budget films, choreographers make $3,000 for a five-day week; in television, $7,500 to $10,000 for up to fourteen workdays.

Words from the Pros

Introducing Mark Marek, Singer and Dance Band Leader

Mark Marek is a singer and the leader of Private Stock Variety Dance Band of Lenexa, Kansas. His background includes two years of college with course work focusing on music theory, audio engineering, and the fundamentals of music and business.

"I started playing the drums in junior high school and then learned how to play the six-string guitar," says Marek. "By the time I was sixteen, my brother had his own band, so I started playing and learning about bands from him. Fourteen years ago, started my own band, which is primarily a country club, high ar–type band. We play mostly at weddings, country clubs, and other formal occasions. The band's working hours are usually 6:30 P.M. until 1 A.M., mostly on Fridays and Saturdays. Most gigs usually last three to four hours, and we must arrive there at least an hour and a half before the start time. We generally do one-hour sets, with a twenty-minute break every hour or so. In addition to setting up, we also have to break down the equipment. But because we've been together for so long, we don't need to rehearse much, perhaps every three to four months.

"I love seeing the reaction of the audience. It's fun to know and see that they are having a good time. That's the thrill I get out of it. What I least like is the inconsistency in bookings. Each month the number of gigs changes, which affects the cash flow. The peak periods for the band are December, May, and June.

"During the week, I mostly take bookings, spend time on the phone getting the specifics for each one, and contact the five band members about our schedule. I also handle all of the contracts for each performance. Aside from the band, I also give private guitar lessons and book gigs for other bands.

"To approach success in the music industry, you need to have good people skills, a general sense of business, a real enjoyment for what you do, a recognition of what your niche is in the music world, patience, good customer relations skills, expert technical skills, and a knowledge of audio and video technology.

"Having a band is a business, not an ego trip. You really need to have a basic knowledge of business and marketing," he stresses. "You can be the best musician, but you have to know how to sell yourself in order to be successful. It's a tough way to make a living—that's why you have to really have a passion for the business."

Introducing Priscilla Gale, Singer and Voice Teacher

Soprano Priscilla Gale attended both the Juilliard School of Music and the Cleveland Institute of Music. She has also studied in Austria and with private teachers Luigi Ricci (in Rome) and

Michael Trimble. Currently, when she's not performing with an opera company or symphony orchestra, she is a faculty member at Wesleyan University in Middletown, Connecticut, where she teaches voice.

"Having come from a very musical family of pianists, singers, and violinists, I was at the piano at the age of five," says Gale. "My family always assumed that I would pursue a career as a pianist, but I realized my real joy and fulfillment was in singing, not the piano. As I began to explore that world more thoroughly, I discovered opera, and I found my home. The rest is history. I received my first professional contract with the Ft. Wayne (Indiana) Symphony Orchestra during my senior year at Cleveland Institute of Music.

"Every engagement a singer or performer experiences changes you in the most wonderful way. You, as an artist, grow on multiple levels, both personally and artistically. Each time, your artistic life is changed; you grow in some immeasurable, wonderful way, and the possibilities are limitless.

"No one job site is like another. In opera, the rehearsals are intense, with the appropriate union breaks but with long, long days, usually over a ten- to twelve-hour period daily and over two weeks or perhaps three. It really depends on how a company works, and they all work differently.

"Orchestra jobs tend to be over a three- or four-day period. Usually you have a piano rehearsal with the conductor, then there are one or two orchestra rehearsals, followed by the performances. It is always busy and intense but exciting. It is fast paced, and one must know one's craft. There is little room for poor preparation. And you must always have the ability to adjust to every circumstance and environment, for no two are ever the same. Every conductor is different, every director, etc. You must be very adaptable and professional.

"What I love most about my work is the ability to touch an audience—people I never meet individually, but collectively. My heart and soul meet theirs. But there are just not enough performance opportunities for everyone, and it is no longer possible to make a full-time living at this career unless you are one of the lucky top 20 percent.

"I always tell people who want to do this kind of work to look inward and ask if there is anything else in life that will bring them happiness and fulfillment. If so, then I suggest that they do that instead. If not, then they should by all means pursue this career. But know that it is—especially in the beginning—a very complicated business that represents a difficult life.

"Talent is but a small piece of it. Most people cannot comprehend the level of sacrifice that this career requires. There is that wonderful, romantic notion of being the 'starving artist,' but there's nothing romantic about it when you're living it.

"However, with hard work, determination, perseverance, and an unwavering faith in yourself, anything can happen. The journey is an incredible ride, and one I would not have missed. And as I look back at my past, at my present, and toward my future, I can honestly say that I am one of the lucky ones."

Introducing Karen Tyler, Singer, Songwriter, and Guitarist

Karen Tyler of Austin, Texas, earned an associate of arts degree from Pepperdine University. She has been working as a blues singer, songwriter, and guitarist since 1979.

"I had a natural talent for singing and found songwriting to be an incredible emotional outlet," says Tyler. "And I have developed some pretty good business skills in order to stay in the music business. From the beginning, being front and center stage and being appreciated for my feelings was important to me.

"Many artists have to have day jobs to support their music, making it very difficult to actually have the time to write, record, and do live performances. My husband and I moved to Texas so that we could afford to live on one salary while I pursued my music. Since he is also my bass player, my studio engineer, producer, and maker and repairer of guitars, he of course benefits from any of my successes.

"I get up fairly early each day and start to work by 9 or 10 A.M.," she says. "I always have so many tasks to accomplish! I keep a mailing list and create all of my own promotional materials via the computer and a couple of printers. I am responsible for all of the bookkeeping and accounting of band income and CD and tape sales. I write a quarterly newsletter. I also make demo tapes and mail out promotional packages almost constantly. I do tons of research on radio stations, booking agents, clubs, festivals, record companies and the like. I read everything about the music business and the blues that I can get my hands on. I spend anywhere from one to four hours a day doing just the business of music. In addition, I play several nights a week from two to four hours, sometimes traveling three and four hours to play. Nothing at all may happen for a period of time, and just when I get into a routine I really like, someone will call or an opportunity will arise that will take all of my attention.

"There is never a time when something like songwriting or practicing guitar doesn't take a back seat to some kind of business duty. I have tried to get a manager but have had some really bad experiences, and at this point in my career I feel that it is better if I retain the control, even if the responsibilities are a bit overwhelming. Everyone always has a suggestion about what you should be doing to help your career. And you can't possibly do everything people suggest, so making an action plan and sticking to it is the best thing. Trying to be organized is my biggest challenge, and getting things down on paper helps.

"I spend anywhere from twenty-five to thirty hours a week doing music business and play anywhere from four to twelve hours a week. I work from a home office and so it gets a little lonely. My husband is moving his office into the home, which I assume will make it a bit better for me. At least I will have someone to bounce some ideas off. Sometimes I really feel like I'm out there all alone.

"I enjoy a good crowd response to my music. It makes it all worthwhile when someone comes up and tells me I have an 'amazing voice' or that I play the guitar well or that a certain song really touched them. The worst part is probably that people don't go out as much as they used to. They are 'programmed' by television, radio, and print media as to what to buy and what to listen to or go to see. They get comfortable going to hear certain acts and until they have heard rave reviews about someone forty or fifty times, they don't make the effort to go and see them. Even when they do, they are liable to slip back into the habit of going where they always go. A side effect is that talent doesn't count as much as who you know and how much fun you are to 'hang out with.'

"On top of that, bands who want to 'make it' are expected to finance their own recordings, put out expensive CDs, and sell literally thousands of them before a record company will consider signing them. This is kind of hard when you are playing for fewer and fewer people every day.

"I would advise those interested in this career to go to college and develop a talent (preferably nonmusical) whereby you can create your own business—computers, catering, consulting. You have to have some way of supporting yourself and coming up with $5,000 to $10,000 every year or two for a CD, and you have to have a flexible schedule so that you can tour and support the CD and work whenever you can."

Introducing Kathryn Maffei, Pianist and Music Director

Kathryn Maffei has been playing the piano for more than forty years. She has ten years of classical training through a concert pianist. "When I started taking piano lessons at eight years old," says Maffei, "I began to entertain my family. Then I performed for family and friend's parties as well as local club and organization events. Quickly it spread to playing the piano for chorus classes in grammar school and high school bands and entertaining for many different kinds of local events, such as proms, fashion or variety shows, plays, and other social functions.

"I got married and took a few years off to raise my family. When my children were of preschool and kindergarten age, I went to school with them and did music classes for their teachers because they did not play the piano or have live music for their classes. I became the church organist in communities in which we lived, and I played for weddings, funerals, and masses.

"Once I was heard by others, it quickly spread to doing parties at hotels, country clubs, and Christmas parties, birthday parties, anniversaries, class reunions, etc. I became music director for a performing arts company in my area, and I have been piano conductor for more than a dozen musical plays such as *Oliver; Annie; Big River; Hello Dolly; Bye Bye Birdie; Peter Pan; You're a Good Man, Charlie Brown;* and *Beauty and the Beast.*

"I have provided the music for local beauty pageants, concerts in the park, and Fourth of July pageants. I have performed for many benefits to raise money for projects in our community, and most recently I played for a religious concert. I have also served as a judge for music talent in our area. Currently, I teach thirty-two private piano students, and I am the church pianist/organist as well.

"I began working at Our Lady of Miracles Catholic School in Gustine, California, a private Catholic school, eight years ago, and I now work three days a week teaching music classes from kindergarten through eighth grade. This came about after the assistant superintendent of schools saw me at work and hired me immediately to do music at her school. Most recently, I was appointed to a visual and performing arts committee to integrate performing arts in the schools in our diocese.

"When designing music programs for children, my main concern is to teach a love for the art of music. I believe this is best accomplished at the earliest age possible. Hopefully, this is a feeling that will stay with the children all their lives, as it did in mine. It is well known that bringing music and liberal arts to students is important on so many levels and ensures a broad and rich education. The arts reinforce social skills, instill positive attitudes and values, and support growth and intellectual enrichment. The arts serve not only to develop personal intellectual growth, but also sharpen judgment and interpersonal decision making. The key is to start with young children, and I know almost no other way to get and keep a small child's attention than with music.

"I truly love children and music and have never regretted my profession because I get so much enjoyment out of it. It is my life's work as much it would be for an accountant who works with numbers and a lawyer who deals with laws! To others I say, 'Go for it if you feel it is in your heart!'"

Introducing Mike Watson, Recording Artist

Mike Watson, head of Watson Entertainment, Inc., is a recording artist at Uniworld Records in Atlanta, Georgia. He attended West Georgia College and majored in music.

"I started playing professionally in 1980 as lead guitarist and harmony singer for a band on the circuit," explains Watson. "I have been fascinated with music as long as I can remember, and I turned that dream into reality with a lot of hard work and perseverance and never settling for second best or taking no for an answer.

"When I'm playing in town, a typical day is the following: I rise about noon and do everyday things like cutting grass, etc. Then, I work at the club from 9 P.M. until 1 or 2 A.M. Entertaining is what I do. Naturally, it is always a party atmosphere. When I go to different states doing shows, it's somewhat similar except I get to see places and people in one day I probably will never meet and maybe never see again.

"I love almost every part of my job and consider myself to be so very fortunate because I am able to do the one thing I love doing most—making a living at making music.

"My least favorite part is dealing with people who had a little too much to drink and every now and then having to deal with less than desirable booking agents who send you to a job that isn't quite what they paint it to be.

"My advice to others is, if you have a genuine dream, never give up! If you know in your heart that you have what it takes to succeed in your chosen profession, go for it!"

Introducing Chris Murphy, Musician, Record Producer, and DJ

Chris Murphy is a professional musician, entertainer, record producer, and entertainment buyer, as well as a part-time disc jockey at a college radio station. He began music lessons as a teenager, and later he attended Berkley College of Music in Boston. His father was also a musician, and Chris often played in bands with him before going on the road with his own band in 1978.

"I don't know how to do anything else," says Murphy. "Music is one of the few things I was good at and could take pride in. As a teenager, I felt that music stood out as something that was fun and that I excelled at. I started playing the saxophone at age seventeen and started playing in bands about the same time. I was in love with the blues long before I became a blues musician.

"My work atmosphere is great; I play in blues clubs four to six nights a week. I also spend at least an hour a day on the phone, organizing gigs and musicians. I meet a lot of interesting, talented, and funny people. I receive a lot of respect and love from the audiences I perform for. There is nothing that can replace the feeling of being onstage with a great band on a good night! I also have time to spend with my daughter in the daytime during the week, though occasionally I am away for the weekend.

"I enjoy the fact that when I go out to earn money, I am going out to play. How many people can say that?

"My advice to others is to never, ever quit. The people who hang in there are the ones who inherit the entertainment business!

Introducing Lionel Ward, Musician

Lionel Ward first became interested in being a musician when he was only nine years old and his mother bought him an Airline guitar for Christmas. Now he tours North America and Europe as the lead singer for the New World Band, a musical group that entertains audiences with classic and contemporary rock and country songs.

Lionel was discovered by the late Wolfman Jack, who noticed Lionel's resemblance to Elvis Presley and invited him to a meeting. (Even now, the band ends each performance with a tribute to Elvis.) Lionel's manager then sent a demo tape to Wolfman Jack's record label, Sonic Records, Inc., and the New World Band began recording under the Sonic label.

"I came from a musical family, so there was always music in the house," Ward says. "Music is therapy for the soul. It is the greatest feeling in the world to be able to play in front of an audience and see the enjoyment you give people. If you can relieve them of the everyday burdens of life for just a few minutes, you've done something important. The natural high you get from doing a live show cannot be compared to anything else. The only way you can achieve this feeling is through the music. And the beautiful thing is that it is all natural. Being able to sing and play an instrument is a God-given talent; you cannot buy this anywhere. You have to be born with it. It is a blessing to be able to share it with your audience.

"One thing I learned very early in the entertainment business is that every performance has to be the best you can possibly do. The key is to be able to sing your songs as if they are being performed for the very first time. It may actually be the thousandth time you have sung that song, but in my opinion, it should be a thousand times better than the first. The people in the audience have chosen to take the time out of their evening to come and hear you play. You do not want to disappoint them, and I always make sure I do my very best, whether there are five people in the audience or five thousand.

"My job as lead singer is to ensure that all arrangements have been made for the band. How big is the stage? How much room do I have to move around? The size of the show will tell us which public address system we are going to use for the evening. What lighting system is going to be used? How many people are we going to need for the road crew? I must ensure that all of this is taken care of because it affects my show tremendously if I cannot hear the band or we can't see because someone forgot to put up a spotlight.

"As far as what work I actually do, I am involved with every aspect, right down to the last microphone sound check. You cannot measure how many hours are involved because some shows take days. If you count the actual rehearsal time, driving to the gigs, set up and tear down times, and sound checks, you would think we were insane. Our lives are devoted to music, but it is a labor of love. Sometimes we are gone from our homes for weeks. Living in hotels, doing radio and television interviews, is not one big party. I am very fortunate because for as long as I have been doing this, I have never considered it work. I truly love what I am doing.

"I particularly enjoy recording in the studio because it's like taking a piece of your life and freezing it in time. But I also love performing live. Again, there is no better feeling in the world than when the audience is wrapped up in your song and you are taking them on a journey. Sometimes I get so involved in the show that when I open my eyes, everyone is standing and cheering with tears in their eyes. It is then that I know they have felt the same things that I have.

"As far as I can see, there is no downside in this business. I am very fortunate that my wife travels with me and shares my dreams. For some people, I think a downside would be having to leave their family.

"My advice to others is to follow your dreams and what you feel in your heart. This business is very rough and unforgiving at times. But if you believe in yourself and you have the burning desire to make it, then you will. This business cannot be measured by hours or even days. It cannot be measured by money, either, though we need money to survive. If you truly believe in yourself and your music, everything else will fall into place.

"Many times you will hear me thank the audience for their support through the years. I was born a poor boy—rich with love and dreams, though—and I am definitely living my dreams!"

Introducing John A. Roberts, DJ and Business Owner

John Roberts attended Montgomery College, Rockville campus, majoring in speech and drama and then attended the University of Maryland at College Park, majoring in radio and television.

In August of 1996, he competed in the National DJ of the Year competition in Atlantic City and ranked in the Top Ten DJs nationally. He was awarded the Best Club DJ of 1996 in Las Vegas by the American DJ Awards. He has spoken at numerous DJ conventions nationally and in Canada and has written articles for magazines such as *Mobile Beat, DJ Times,* and the *ADJA News.*

"I started as a stand-up comic in the late sixties to mid-seventies," says Roberts. "As I was one of the first in this profession, I learned from the 'school of hard knocks.' While in the Air Force I competed in the AF talent show, the Tops in Blue competition. I won first place in comedy and went on to worldwide competition.

"Currently I am owner of John Roberts' Roving Records—my personal DJ and karaoke service. I am also founder and National Operations Manager of the American Disc Jockey Association and owner of The DJ Training Center—the nation's first full-service independent training facility.

"I started as a DJ while still in the air force, at the USO club in Washington, D.C., in 1973.

"In 1975, when I was about to get out of the service, I had this totally unique idea. By acting as DJ and playing records, I would serve as a band for clubs, weddings, and other parties. I could go anywhere and be *mobile!* I had absolutely *no* idea that someone else might have this idea, too. I certainly had never heard of it and knew of no one who did it. Many people close to me thought I was crazy and should pursue a real job. No one knew disco was brewing right around the corner. That's when DJs truly became accepted as a form of entertainment.

"I always wanted to get into broadcasting and wanted to keep up with my comedy. But after doing stand-up comedy and doing stage shows in high school and college, I loved the live audience. I figured being a mobile DJ could be a stepping-stone in both directions.

"In radio you played to a wall. In a club or party, I was playing to live people and could feel the people and see their instant reaction to things I did. It was totally spontaneous. This is what attracted me to this particular format of entertainment. I could be self-employed and fulfill the American dream doing something I really loved. How many people can say that every time they work—it's a party!

"But it's also a business and must be treated as such. We deal with contracts so there are legal issues that must be put in order. There is a lot of responsibility involved. Music and supplies must be ordered and maintained. Keeping up with music is a major expense. These are the tools of the trade. Equipment must be purchased and maintained. There are promotions, marketing, advertising, hiring, firing, bookkeeping, and all the other normal procedures that any office or business encompasses.

"My days are busy. I am responsible for answering phones and handling customer inquiries, performing the negotiations and attending to contracts, training and scheduling DJs, ordering supplies and music, promoting the business, making advertising decisions, cataloging music, and creating and printing our karaoke catalogs.

"Then at night I will perform at a party. This requires more than just playing music. DJs work as coordinators between the host and guests. We take requests from party goers and, in general, try to keep everyone involved and happy.

"What I like most about this career is that I am my own boss. I can pick and choose the shows I do. I get to work in exciting places and meet exciting, sometimes famous people. Being a mobile DJ has lead to some interesting job opportunities for me. I did a television show like *American Bandstand* for more than three years. I was a part of more than thirty to forty radio and television commercials, performed on radio, served as one of the original hosts of the Home Shopper's Club of Virginia, auditioned for a movie, and have been able to travel all over the United States.

"On the downside, there are no benefits that you ordinarily receive from an employer (unless you are willing to pay for them). It's very hard on my personal social life. My average time to get to sleep is three or four in the morning.

"My advice is that people should realize that this is a business and that it must be treated as such. I'd advise others never to burn bridges. Create friendly competitors and network, network, network. Learn to entertain, to think on your feet. Always be willing to learn new tricks and techniques to stay on top. The minute you think you know it all is the minute your competition starts getting ahead of you."

Introducing Sean M. Meaney, Musician and Business Owner

Sean Meaney is owner of Sterling Entertainment of Tempe, Arizona. He entered the music business in 1984.

"When I first started doing this," Meaney says, "I couldn't believe that people would pay me to perform at parties. (Of course, I was only fifteen at the time.) A few years later, I got my first chance to work in a nightclub. With people asking me to do private parties, it just took off. The hardest part was learning about equipment. I did not go to school for any technical training, so it was all done by trial and error.

"After fourteen years, my love for performing has evolved into a company that performs at weddings, bar or bas mitzvahs, and corporate events. And I still learn new things every day.

"We are one of the few DJ/entertainment companies that do this full-time. During the week, there is a lot of office work, which involves booking jobs, going to meet clients, and finding new ways to entertain people. For me, a typical day begins in the office, working on different marketing ideas. If there are no clients to see, I continue to pursue these efforts all day. On Friday we get ready for the weekend. That includes getting all of the equipment ready for the DJs. We want to make sure that everything is all set.

"Some seasons are busier than others. The wedding season is always a hectic one. Besides running the office, I still go out to do shows. All together, I put in about sixty plus hours per week.

"My favorite part of this job remains my love for entertaining. And I enjoy working for myself. On the downside, it is very difficult to find reliable people to hire to do shows. Also, running your own company is not easy.

"My advice to others is to set your goals and stick to that path. There are many areas in this business to go into—just pick one and proceed!"

For More Information

There are literally hundreds of professional associations for musicians and dancers. Contact any of the following for more information about employment in this field:

American Choral Directors Association (ACDA)
P.O. Box 6310
Lawton, OK 73506

American Federation of Musicians (AFM)
1501 Broadway, Suite 600
New York, NY 10036

American Federation of Television and Radio Artists (AFTRA)
260 Madison Avenue
New York, NY 10016

American Guild of Musical Artists (AGMA)
1727 Broadway
New York, NY 10019

American Guild of Organists (AGO)
475 Riverside Drive, Suite 1260
New York, NY 10115

American Guild of Music (AGM)
5354 Washington Street, Box 3
Downers Grove, IL 60515

American Federation of Musicians
1501 Broadway, Suite 600
New York, NY 10036

American Music Conference (AMC)
5140 Avenida Encinas
Carlsbad, CA 92008

American Musicological Society
201 South Thirty-fourth Street
University of Pennsylvania
Philadelphia, PA 19104

American Symphony Orchestra League (ASOL)
777 Fourteenth Street NW, Suite 500
Washington, DC 20005

Academy of Country Music (ACM)
500 Sunnyside Boulevard
Woodbury, NY 11797

Association of Canadian Orchestras
56 The Esplanade, Suite 311
Toronto, Ontario M5EIA7
CANADA

Black Music Association (BMA)
1775 Broadway
New York, NY 10019

Broadcast Education Association
National Association of Broadcasters
1771 N Street NW
Washington, DC 20036

Broadcast Music, Inc. (BMI)
320 West Fifty-seventh Street
New York, NY 10019

Chamber Music America
545 Eighth Avenue
New York, NY 10018

Chorus America
Association of Professional Vocal Ensembles
2111 Sansom Street
Philadelphia, PA 19103

College Music Society
202 West Spruce
Missoula, MT 59802

Concert Artists Guild (CAG)
850 Seventh Avenue, Room 1003
New York, NY 10019

Country Music Association (CMA)
P.O. Box 22299
One Music Circle South
Nashville, TN 37203

Gospel Music Association (GMA)
P.O. Box 23201
Nashville, TN 37202

International Conference of Symphony and Opera Musicians
    (ICSOM)
6607 Waterman
St. Louis, MO 63130

Metropolitan Opera Association (MOA)
Lincoln Center
New York NY 10023

National Academy of Popular Music (NAPM)
885 Second Avenue
New York, NY 10017

National Academy of Recording Arts and Sciences (NARAS)
303 North Glen Oaks Boulevard, Suite 140
Burbank, CA 91502

National Association of Music Theaters
John F. Kennedy Center for the Performing Arts
Washington, DC 20566

National Association of Schools of Music
11250 Roger Bacon Drive, Suite 21
Reston, VA 22091

National Orchestral Association (NOA)
474 Riverside Drive, Room 455
New York, NY 10115

National Symphony Orchestra Association (NSOA)
John F. Kennedy Center for the Performing Arts
Washington, DC 20566

Opera America
777 Fourteenth Street NW, Suite 520
Washington, DC 20005

Radio-Television News Directors Association
1717 K Street NW, Suite 615
Washington, DC 20006

Society of Professional Audio Recording Studios
4300 Tenth Avenue North, #2
Lake Worth, FL 33461

Screen Actors Guild (SAG)
7065 Hollywood Boulevard
Hollywood, CA 90028

Touring Entertainment Industry Association (TEIA)
1203 Lake Street
Fort Worth, TX 76102

Women in Music
P.O. Box 441
Radio City Station
New York, NY 10101

For information on purchasing directories about colleges and universities that teach dance, including details on the types of courses offered, and available scholarships, write to:

National Dance Association
1900 Association Drive
Reston, VA 22091

A directory of dance, art and design, music, and theater programs may be purchased from:

National Association of Schools of Dance
11250 Roger Bacon Drive, Suite 21
Reston, VA 22090

For information on all aspects of dance, including job listings, send a self-addressed stamped envelope to:

American Dance Guild
31 West Twenty-first Street, Third Floor
New York, NY 10010

A directory of dance companies and related organizations, plus other information on professional dance, is available from:

Dance/USA
777 Fourteenth Street NW, Suite 540
Washington, DC 20005

CHAPTER FOUR

Careers in Sales

The capitalist system does not guarantee that everybody will become rich, but it guarantees that anybody can become rich.
RAUL R. deSALES

HELP WANTED: We are a provider of medical, scientific, and technology research information to academic, corporate, and government markets. Our company is seeking a western region field sales rep. Responsibilities include maintaining customer databases, generating and qualifying sales leads, negotiating sales agreements, representing the company at trade shows, and preparing weekly sales reports. The position requires 50 percent travel. Our ideal candidate will have a four-year college degree with a minimum of three years of outside sales experience, preferably within the information industry. We are looking for a self-motivated, organized individual who has a working knowledge of the Internet, excellent verbal and written communication skills, and computer literacy. We offer a highly competitive compensation package inclusive of medical/dental coverage and a 401k plan. Please send cover letter, resume, and salary history to us via the following fax number.

Does the job described in this want ad hold appeal for you? It represents only one of a broad range of possibilities in this field. Many extroverts find their special niche in the world of sales, helping meet the needs of consumers in as many ways as there are products or services to sell.

Zeroing in on What
Sales Professionals Do

Sales professionals must know how to interact well with others in order to ascertain what potential buyers' needs and desires are and how they can best be met. The better that salespeople know their product, and the more at ease they are with others, the more successful they will be in their sales careers. Sales offers many opportunities in a range of positions, products and services, businesses and industries, and locations.

For this book, general sales is broken into the following primary categories:

• Retail

• Services

• Manufacturing and Wholesale

Industry-specific sales careers in insurance, real estate, and travel are also covered in this chapter.

Retail Sales

Millions of dollars are spent each day on all types of merchandise—everything from sweaters and books to food and furniture.

Whether selling clothing, cosmetics, or automobiles, a sales worker's primary job is to interest customers in the merchandise. This may be done by describing the product's features, demonstrating its use, showing various models and colors, and pointing out why products will benefit the customer or client.

For some jobs, particularly those involving the selling of expensive and complex items, special knowledge or skills are needed. For example, workers who sell personal computers must be able to explain to customers the features of various brands and models, the meaning of manufacturers' specifications, and the types of software that are available.

In other jobs that require selling standardized articles—food, hardware, linens, and housewares, for example—sales workers may often do little more than take payments and bag purchases.

Some retail sales workers also receive cash, check, and charge payments; handle returns; and give change and receipts. Depending on the hours they work, they may have to open or close the cash register. This may include counting the money in the cash register; separating charge slips, coupons, and exchange vouchers; and making deposits at the cash office. Sales workers are often held responsible for the contents of their registers and, in many organizations, repeated shortages are cause for dismissal.

In addition, sales workers may help stock shelves or racks, arrange for mailing or delivery of a purchase, mark price tags, take inventory, and prepare displays.

Sales workers must be aware of not only the promotions their stores are sponsoring, but also those that are being sponsored by competitors. Also, they often must recognize possible security risks and know how to handle such situations.

Consumers often form their impressions of a store by its sales force. The retail industry is very competitive and, increasingly, employers are stressing the importance of providing courteous and efficient service. When a customer wants a product that is not on the sales floor, for example, the sales worker may check the stockroom and, if there are none there, place a special order or call another store to locate the item.

Job Settings for Retail Sales Workers

Sales workers are employed by many types of retailers to assist customers in the selection and purchase of merchandise. The largest employers of retail sales workers are department stores. Other types of employers include specialty shops and boutiques and independently owned stores as well as large chain outlets such as those selling hardware or office supplies.

Catalog and on-line sales are two more large areas that provide additional avenues for those interested in venturing into retail sales as a career.

Qualifications and Training for Retail Sales Workers

Usually, there are no formal education requirements for working in sales. However, employers still prefer candidates with some schooling and work experience. They also seek out those who enjoy interacting with people and those who have the tact and patience to deal with difficult customers. Among other desirable characteristics are an interest in sales work, a neat appearance, and the ability to communicate clearly and effectively.

Before hiring a candidate, some employers may conduct a background check, especially for jobs in selling high-priced items.

In most small stores, an experienced employee or the proprietor instructs newly hired sales personnel in making out sales checks and operating the cash register. In larger stores, training programs are more formal and usually are conducted over several days.

As salespeople gain experience and seniority, they usually move to positions of greater responsibility and are given their choice of departments. This often means moving to areas with potentially higher earnings and commissions. The highest earnings potential is usually found in selling big-ticket items. This work often requires the most knowledge of the product and the greatest talent for persuasion.

Years ago, capable sales workers without a college degree could advance to management positions, but today, large retail businesses generally prefer to hire college graduates as management trainees, making a college education increasingly important.

Despite this trend, capable employees without a college degree may be able to advance to administrative or supervisory work in large stores.

In small stores, opportunities for advancement vary. In some cases, advancement opportunities are limited because one person, often the owner, does most of the managerial work. In others, however, some sales workers are promoted to assistant managers.

Retail selling experience may be an asset when applying for sales positions with larger retailers or in other industries, such as financial services, wholesale trade, or manufacturing.

Compensation for Retail Sales

The starting salary for many part-time retail sales positions is the federal minimum wage. In some areas where employers are having difficulty attracting and retaining workers, wages will be higher than the established minimum.

The following chart shows average weekly earnings by class of sales worker in several industries.

Motor vehicle and boat—$479

Radio, television, hi-fi, and appliance—$415

Furniture and home furnishings—$354

Hardware and building supplies—$323

Parts—$319

Apparel—$255

Compensation systems vary by type of establishment and merchandise sold. Some sales workers receive an hourly wage. Others receive a commission or a combination of wages and commissions. Under a commission system, salespeople receive a percentage of the sales they make. This offers sales workers the opportunity to significantly increase their earnings, but they may find their earnings depend as much on the ups and downs in the economy as on their ability to sell their products.

In addition, nearly all sales workers are able to buy their store's merchandise at a discount, often from 10 to 40 percent below regular prices. In some cases, this privilege is extended to the employees' families as well.

Services Sales

Services sales representatives are involved in selling a wide variety of services. For example, sales representatives for data processing services firms sell complex services such as inventory control, payroll processing, sales analysis, and financial reporting systems. Hotel sales representatives contact government, business, and social groups to solicit convention and conference business for the hotel. Fund-raisers plan programs to raise money for charities or other nonprofit causes. Sales representatives for temporary help services firms locate and acquire clients who will hire the firms' employees.

Telephone services sales representatives visit commercial customers to review their telephone systems, analyze their communications needs, and recommend services such as installation of additional equipment. Other representatives sell automotive leasing, public utility, burial, shipping, protective, and management consulting services.

Services sales representatives act as industry experts, consultants, and problem solvers when selling their firm's services. The sales representative, in some cases, creates demand for his or her firm's services. A prospective client who is asked to consider buying a particular service may never have used, or even been aware of a need for, that service. For example, wholesalers might be persuaded to order a list of credit ratings for checking their customers' credit records prior to making sales and discover that the list could be used to solicit new business.

There are several different categories of services sales jobs. *Outside sales representatives* call on clients and prospects at their homes or offices. They may make appointments, or they may practice "cold calls," arriving without any prior notice. *Inside sales representatives* work on their employers' premises, assisting individuals interested in the firms' services. *Telemarketing sales representatives* sell exclusively over the telephone. They make large numbers of calls to prospects, attempting to sell the service themselves or to arrange an appointment between the prospect and an outside sales representative. Some sales representatives deal exclusively with one, or a few, major clients.

Despite the diversity of services being sold, the jobs of all services sales representatives have much in common. All sales representatives must fully understand and be able to discuss the services their companies offer.

Also, the procedures they follow are similar. Many sales representatives develop lists of prospective clients through telephone and business directories, asking business associates and customers for leads, and calling on new businesses as they cover their assigned territory. Some services sales representatives acquire clients through client inquiries about the company's services.

Regardless of how they first meet the client, all services sales representatives must explain how the services being offered can meet the clients' needs. This often involves demonstrations of the company's services. Sales reps must answer questions about the nature and cost of the services and try to overcome objections in order to persuade potential customers to purchase the services. If they fail to make a sale on the first visit, they may follow up with more visits, letters, or phone calls. After closing a sale, services sales representatives generally follow up to see that the purchase meets the customer's needs and to determine if additional services can be sold.

Because services sales representatives obtain many of their new accounts through referrals, their success hinges on developing a satisfied clientele who will continue to use the services and will recommend them to other potential customers. Like other types of sales jobs, a services sales representative's reputation is crucial to his or her success.

Services sales work varies with the kind of service sold. Selling highly technical services, such as communications systems or computer consulting services, involves complex and lengthy sales negotiations. In addition, sales of such complex services may require extensive after-sale support. In these situations, sales representatives may operate as part of a team of sales representatives and experts from other departments. Sales representatives receive valuable technical assistance from these experts. For example, those who sell data processing services might work with a systems engineer or computer scientist, and those who sell telephone services might receive technical assistance from a communications consultant. Teams enhance customer service and build strong long-term relationships with customers, resulting in increased sales.

Because of the length of time between the initial contact with a customer and the actual sale, representatives who sell complex technical services generally work with several customers simultaneously. Sales representatives must be well organized and efficient in scheduling their time.

Selling less complex services, such as linen supply or exterminating services, generally involves simpler and shorter sales negotiations.

A sales representative's job may likewise vary with the size of the employer. Those working for large companies generally are more specialized and are assigned territorial boundaries, a specific line of services, and their own accounts. In smaller companies, sales representatives may have broader responsibilities: administrative, marketing, or public relations, for example, in addition to their sales duties.

Job Settings for Services Sales Representatives

Services sales representatives hold more than half a million jobs nationwide. More than half of these jobs are in firms providing business services, including computer and data processing, advertising, personnel supply, equipment rental and leasing, mailing, reproduction, and stenographic services.

Other sales representatives work for firms that offer a wide range of other services, such as engineering and management, personal, amusement and recreation, automotive repair, membership organizations, hotels, motion pictures, health, and education services.

Qualifications and Training for Services Sales Representatives

Many employers require services sales representatives to have college degrees, but requirements may vary depending on the industry a particular company represents. Employers who market advertising services seek individuals with college degrees in advertising or marketing or master's degrees in business administration; companies that market educational services prefer individuals with advanced degrees in marketing or related fields.

Many hotels seek graduates from college hotel administration programs, and companies that sell computer services and telephone systems prefer sales representatives with computer science or engineering backgrounds.

College courses in business, economics, communications, and marketing are helpful in obtaining other jobs as services sales representatives.

Employers may hire experienced, high-performing sales representatives who have only a high school diploma, and this is particularly true for those who sell nontechnical services, such as exterminating, laundry, or funeral services.

Many firms conduct intensive training programs for their sales representatives. A sound training program covers the history of the business; origin, development, and uses of the service; effective prospecting methods; presentation of the service; answering customer complaints; creating customer demand; closing a sale; writing an order; company policies; and using technical support personnel.

Sales representatives also may attend seminars on a wide range of subjects given by in-house or outside training institutions. These sessions acquaint employees with new services and products and help them maintain and update their sales techniques and may include motivational or sensitivity training to make sales representatives more effective in dealing with people. Sales staffs often receive training in the use of computers and communications technology in order to increase their productivity.

In order to be successful, sales representatives should be pleasant, outgoing, and have good rapport with people. They must be highly motivated, well organized, and efficient. Good grooming and a neat appearance are essential, as are self-confidence, reliability, and the ability to communicate effectively. Sales representatives should be self-starters who have the ability to work under pressure to meet sales goals. Those who have good sales records and leadership ability may advance to supervisory and managerial positions. Frequent contact with businesspeople in other firms provides sales workers with leads about job openings, enhancing advancement opportunities.

Compensation for Services Sales

The median annual income for full-time advertising sales representatives is about $26,000. Representatives selling other types of business services earn about $30,200. Earnings of representatives who sell technical services generally are higher than earnings of those who sold nontechnical services.

The average yearly income for entry-level technical services sales is about $36,000, ranging up to $63,000 for senior sales staff.

Earnings of experienced sales representatives depend on performance. Successful sales representatives who establish a strong customer base can earn more than managers in their firms. Some sales representatives earn well over $100,000 a year.

Sales representatives work on different types of compensation plans. Some get a straight salary; others are paid solely on a commission basis—a percentage of the dollar value of their sales. Most firms use a combination of salary and commissions.

Some services sales representatives receive a base salary plus incentive pay that adds 50 to 70 percent to the base salary. In addition to the same benefits package received by other employees of the firm, outside sales representatives have expense accounts to cover meals and travel and, in some cases, a company car. Many employers offer bonuses—including vacation time, trips, and prizes—for sales that exceed company quotas.

In spite of all the perks, earnings may vary widely from year to year with fluctuating economic conditions and consumer and business expectations.

Manufacturers' and Wholesale Sales

Articles of clothing, books, and computers are among the thousands of products bought and sold each day. Manufacturers' and wholesale sales representatives play an important role in this process. While retail sales workers sell products directly to customers, manufacturers' representatives market their products to other manufacturers, wholesale and retail establishments, government agencies, and other institutions. Regardless of the types of products they sell, the primary duties of these sales representatives are to interest wholesale and retail buyers and purchasing agents in their merchandise and ensure that any questions or concerns of current clients are addressed. Manufacturers' and wholesale ales reps also provide advice to clients on how to increase their own sales.

Depending on where they work, these sales representatives have different job titles. Many of those representing manufacturers are referred to as manufacturers' representatives, and those employed by wholesalers generally are called sales representatives. Those selling technical products, for both manufacturers and wholesalers, are usually called industrial sales workers or sales engineers. In addition to those employed directly by firms, manufacturers' agents are self-employed sales workers who contract their services to all types of companies.

Manufacturers' and wholesale sales representatives spend much of their time traveling to and visiting with prospective buyers and current clients. During a sales call, they discuss the customers' needs and suggest how their merchandise or services can meet those needs. They may show samples or catalogs and inform customers about prices, availability, and how their products can save money and improve productivity. In addition, because of the vast number of manufacturers and wholesalers selling similar products, they try to beat the competition by emphasizing the unique qualities of the products and services offered by their companies. They also take orders and resolve any problems or complaints with the merchandise.

These sales representatives have additional duties as well. For example, sales engineers, who are among the most highly trained sales workers, typically sell products whose installation and optimal use require technical expertise and support, products such as material handling equipment, numerical-control machinery, and computer systems.

In addition to providing information on their firms' products, these workers help prospective and current buyers with technical problems. For example, they may recommend improved materials and machinery for a firm's manufacturing process, draw up plans of proposed machinery layouts, and estimate cost savings from the use of their equipment. They gather and present this information and negotiate the sale, which may take several months.

Sales engineers must also provide follow-up services, keeping in close contact with the client to assure that he or she renews the contract. Sales engineers may work with engineers in their own companies, adapting products to a customer's special needs.

Increasingly, sales representatives who lack technical expertise work as part of a team with a technical expert. For example, a sales representative will make the preliminary contact with customers, introduce his or her company's product, and close the sale. However, the technically trained person will attend the sales presentation to explain and answer technical questions and concerns. In this way, the sales representative is able to spend more time maintaining and soliciting accounts and less time acquiring technical knowledge.

Obtaining new accounts is an important part of the job. Sales representatives follow leads suggested by other clients, from advertisements in trade journals, and from participation in trade shows and conferences. At times, they make unannounced visits to potential clients. In addition, they may spend a lot of time meeting with and entertaining prospective clients during evenings and weekends.

Sales representatives also analyze sales statistics, prepare reports, and handle administrative duties, such as filing their expense account reports, scheduling appointments, and making travel plans. They study literature about new and existing products and monitor the sales, prices, and products of their competitors.

In addition to all these duties, manufacturers' agents must manage their businesses. This requires organizational skills as well as knowledge of accounting, marketing, and administration.

Some manufacturers' and wholesale sales representatives have large territories and do considerable traveling. Because a sales region may cover several states, they may be away from home for several days or weeks at a time. Others work near a home base and do most of their traveling by automobile. Because of the nature of the work and the amount of travel, sales representatives typically work more than forty hours per week.

The daily activities of sales reps are tracked by supervisors—where they have been, who they have seen, and what they have sold.

Sales Managers

Sales managers direct the firm's sales programs. They assign sales territories and goals and establish training programs for their sales representatives. Managers advise their sales representatives on ways to improve their sales performance. In large, multi-product firms, they oversee regional and local sales managers and their staffs. Sales managers maintain contact with dealers and distributors. They analyze sales statistics gathered by their staffs to determine sales potential and inventory requirements and monitor the preferences of customers. Such information is vital to develop new products and maximize profits.

Sales managers also have to go out in the field to see their sales reps. They make sure the reps are using the right techniques and handling each situation the way it should be handled in order to get the maximum sales volume. The reps can't afford to take the time to come to the office and lose sales.

Qualifications and Training for Manufacturers' and Wholesale Sales Representatives

The background needed for sales jobs varies by product line and market. As the number of college graduates has increased and the job requirements have become more technical and analytical, most firms have placed a greater emphasis on a strong educational background. Nevertheless, many employers still hire individuals with previous sales experience who do not have college degrees. In fact, in some cases, sales ability, personality, and familiarity with brands are more important than a degree.

On the other hand, firms selling industrial products often require a degree in science or engineering in addition to some sales experience. In general, companies are looking for the best and brightest individuals who display the personality and desire necessary to sell.

Many companies have formal training programs that last up to two years for beginning sales representatives. However, most businesses are accelerating these programs to reduce costs and expedite the return from training. In some programs, trainees rotate among jobs in plants and offices to learn all phases of production, installation, and distribution of the product. In others, trainees take formal classroom instruction at the plant, followed by on-the-job training under the supervision of a field sales manager.

In some firms, new workers are trained by accompanying more experienced workers on their sales calls. As these workers gain familiarity with the firms' products and clients, they are given increasing responsibility until they are eventually assigned their own territory. As businesses experience greater competition, increased pressure is placed upon sales representatives to produce faster.

These workers must stay abreast of new merchandise and the changing needs of their customers. They may attend trade shows where new products are displayed or conferences and conventions where they meet with other sales representatives and clients to discuss new product developments. In addition, many companies sponsor meetings for the entire sales force where presentations are made on sales performance, product development, and profitability.

Sales representatives should enjoy traveling because much of their time is spent visiting current and prospective clients.

Compensation for Manufacturers' and Wholesale Sales

Compensation methods vary significantly by the type of firm and product sold. However, most employers use a combination of salary and commission or salary plus bonus. Commissions are usually based on the amount of sales, whereas bonuses may depend on individual performance, on the performance of all sales workers in the group or district, or on the company's overall performance.

Median annual earnings of full-time manufacturers' and wholesale sales representatives is about $36,000, although some might start out as low as $16,000 and range up to $62,000 or more per year. Earnings vary by experience and the type of products sold.

In addition to their earnings, sales representatives are usually reimbursed for expenses such as transportation costs, meals, hotels, and entertaining customers. They often receive benefits such as health and life insurance, a pension plan, vacation and sick leave, personal use of a company car, and frequent flyer mileage. Some companies offer incentives such as free vacation trips or gifts for outstanding sales workers.

Unlike those working directly for a manufacturer or wholesaler, manufacturers' agents work strictly on commission. Depending on the type of product they are selling, their experience in the field, and the number of clients, their earnings can be significantly higher or lower than those working in direct sales. In addition, because manufacturers' agents are self-employed, they must pay their own travel and entertainment expenses as well as provide for their own benefits, which can be a significant cost.

Frequently, promotion takes the form of an assignment to a larger account or territory where commissions are likely to be greater. Experienced sales representatives may move into jobs as sales trainers, who train new employees on selling techniques and company policies and procedures. Those who have good sales records and leadership ability may advance to sales supervisor or district manager.

In addition to advancement opportunities within a firm, some go into business for themselves as manufacturers' agents. Others find opportunities in buying, purchasing, advertising, or marketing research. For many sales reps, the end goal is to climb the ladder in sales and transfer into marketing.

Insurance Sales

Insurance agents and brokers sell individuals and businesses insurance policies that provide protection against loss. Policies cover medical, life, automobiles, jewelry, personal valuables, furniture, household items, businesses, real estate, and other properties.

Agents and brokers prepare reports, maintain records, and, in the event of a loss, help policyholders settle insurance claims. Specialists in group policies may help an employer provide employees the opportunity to buy insurance through payroll deductions. Insurance agents may work for one insurance company or as independent agents selling for several companies. Insurance brokers do not sell for a particular company but put into place insurance policies for their clients with the company that offers the best rate and coverage.

Life insurance agents and brokers also are sometimes called life underwriters. Property/casualty insurance agents and brokers sell policies that protect individuals and businesses from financial

loss as a result of automobile accidents, fire, theft, or other property losses. Property/casualty insurance can also cover workers'
compensation, product liability, or medical malpractice. Many
life and property/casualty insurance agents also sell health insurance policies covering the costs of hospital and medical care or
loss of income due to illness or injury.

Because insurance sales agents obtain many new accounts
through referrals, it is important that agents maintain regular
contact with their clients to ensure their financial needs are
being met as personal and business needs change. Developing a
satisfied clientele who will recommend an agent's services to
other potential customers is a key to success in this field.

Qualifications and Training for Insurance Salespeople

For jobs selling insurance, companies prefer college graduates,
particularly those who have majored in business or economics.
Some hire high school graduates with potential or proven sales
ability or who have been successful in other types of work. In
fact, most entrants to agent and broker jobs transfer from other
occupations, so they tend to be older, on average, than entrants
to many other occupations.

Many colleges and universities offer courses in insurance, and
some schools offer a bachelor's degree in insurance. College
courses in finance, mathematics, accounting, economics, business law, government, and business administration enable insurance agents or brokers to understand how social, marketing, and
economic conditions relate to the insurance industry. Courses in
psychology, sociology, and public speaking can prove useful in
improving sales techniques.

It is important for insurance agents and brokers to keep current with issues concerning clients. Changes in tax laws, government benefit programs, and other state and federal regulations
can affect the insurance needs of clients and how agents conduct

business. In addition, some basic familiarity with computers is very important. The use of computers to provide instantaneous information on a wide variety of financial products has greatly improved agents' and brokers' efficiency and enabled them to devote more time to clients.

All insurance agents and brokers must obtain a license in the states in which they plan to sell insurance. In most states, licenses are issued only to applicants who complete specified courses and then pass written examinations covering insurance fundamentals and the state insurance laws.

New agents usually receive training at the agencies where they work and, frequently, also at the insurance company's home office. Beginners sometimes attend company-sponsored classes to prepare for examinations. Others study on their own and accompany experienced agents when they call on prospective clients.

Insurance agents and brokers need to be enthusiastic, outgoing, self-confident, disciplined, hard working, and able to communicate effectively. They should be able to inspire customer confidence. Some companies give personality tests to prospective employees because personality attributes are so important in sales work. Since agents and brokers usually work without supervision, they must be able to plan their time well and have the initiative to locate new clients.

An insurance agent who shows sales ability and leadership may become a sales manager in a local office. A few professionals will advance to agency superintendent or executive positions. However, many who have built a good clientele prefer to remain in sales work. Some, particularly in the property/casualty field, establish their own independent agencies or brokerage firms.

Compensation for Insurance Sales
The median annual earnings of salaried insurance sales workers is about $31,000, but workers can start as low as in the teens and range up to $75,000 a year or more.

Most independent agents are paid on a commission-only basis. Sales workers who are employees of an agency may be paid in one of three ways: salary only, salary plus commission, or salary plus bonus. Commissions, however, are the most common form of compensation, especially for experienced agents. The amount of the commission depends on the type and amount of insurance sold and whether the transaction is a new policy or a renewal. Bonuses are usually awarded when agents meet their production goals or when an agency's profit goals are met. Many agencies also pay for automobile and transportation expenses, conventions and meetings, promotion and marketing expenses, and retirement plans.

All agents are legally responsible for any mistakes they make, and independent agents must purchase their own insurance to cover damages from their errors and omissions.

Real Estate Sales

Buying or selling a home or an investment property is not only one of the most important financial events in peoples' lives but one of the most complex transactions as well. As a result, people generally seek the help of real estate agents or brokers.

Real estate agents and brokers need to have a thorough knowledge of the housing market in their communities. They must know which neighborhoods will best fit their clients' needs and budgets. They have to be familiar with local zoning and tax laws and know where to obtain financing.

Agents and brokers also act as intermediaries for price negotiations between buyer and seller.

Brokers

Brokers are independent businesspeople who, for a fee, sell real estate owned by others. They also rent and manage properties. In closing sales, brokers often provide buyers with information on loans to finance their purchases. They also arrange for title searches and for meetings between buyers and sellers when details of the transactions are agreed upon and the new owners take possession. A broker's knowledge, resourcefulness, and creativity in arranging financing that is most favorable to the prospective buyer often mean the difference between success and failure in closing a sale.

In some cases, agents assume the responsibilities in closing sales, but, in many areas, this is done by lawyers, lenders, or title companies. Brokers also manage their own offices, supervise associate agents, advertise properties, and handle other business matters.

Agents

Real estate agents generally are independent sales workers who provide their services to a licensed broker on a contract basis. In return, the broker pays the agent a portion of the commission earned from property sold through the firm by the agent. Today, relatively few agents receive salaries as employees of a broker or realty firm. Instead, most derive their incomes solely from commissions.

Responsibilities

When you work with customers in real estate, the most important thing is to learn how to listen to what their needs are. Clients will have their dream home in mind with their wish list, telling you everything they want, but often it's not what they can afford. You have to go through the list and help clients identify their priorities. Is it necessary for them to have four bedrooms, for example, or will three do? Do they want one story or two? Do they need a room to serve as an office?

At that point, the agent or broker calls in a mortgage broker and they go through the buyers' qualifications and see where they sit financially. It's very important to prequalify buyers. You can then see if they can afford a $100,000 house, for example, or something more or less costly.

Then you go to the computer and pull up everything that's in that price range. You pick out the most viable possibilities in their price range, start from the top, and work your way down. It's a progression, and often you have to eliminate many things.

Then, the house hunting begins. Agents spend a lot of time showing homes to prospective buyers. Once a home has been found and the contract has been signed by both parties, the real estate broker or agent must see to it that all special terms of the contract are met before the closing date. For example, if the seller has agreed to a home inspection or a termite and radon inspection, the agent must make sure that this is done. Also, if the seller has agreed to any repairs, the broker or agent must see to it that they have been made; otherwise, the sale cannot be completed.

Increasingly, brokers and agents must handle environmental problems or make sure the property they are selling meets environmental regulations. For example, they may be responsible for dealing with problems such as lead paint on the walls. While many other details are handled by loan officers, attorneys, or other people, the agents must check to make sure that these details are completed.

Because brokers and agents must have properties to sell, they spend a significant amount of time obtaining listings (owner agreements to place properties for sale with the firm). When listing property for sale, agents and brokers make comparisons with similar properties that have been sold recently to determine a house's fair market value. Much time is spent on the telephone, exploring leads gathered from various sources, including personal contacts.

Most real estate agents and brokers sell residential property. A few, usually those from large firms or specialized small firms, sell commercial, industrial, agricultural, or other types of real estate.

Each specialty requires knowledge of that particular type of property and clientele.

Although real estate agents and brokers generally work in offices, much of their time is spent outside the office showing properties to customers, analyzing properties for sale, meeting with prospective clients, researching the state of the market, inspecting properties for appraisal, and performing a wide range of other duties. Brokers provide office space, but agents generally furnish their own automobiles.

Qualifications and Training for Real Estate Agents and Brokers

All states and the District of Columbia require real estate agents and brokers to be licensed. This means that every prospective agent must be a high school graduate, be at least eighteen years old, and pass a written test. The examination, which is more comprehensive for brokers than for agents, includes questions on basic real estate transactions and on laws affecting the sale of property.

Most states require candidates for the general sales license to complete at least thirty hours of classroom instruction, and those seeking the broker's license must complete ninety hours of formal training in addition to a specified amount of experience in selling real estate (generally one to three years). Some states waive the experience requirements for the broker's license for applicants who have a bachelor's degree in real estate. A small but increasing number of states require that agents have sixty hours of college credit, roughly the equivalent of an associate's degree.

State licenses generally must be renewed every year or two, usually without reexamination. Many states, however, require continuing education for license renewal.

Personality traits are as important as formal credentials. Brokers look for applicants who possess a pleasant personality, honesty, and a neat appearance. Maturity, tact, and enthusiasm for the job are required in order to motivate prospective customers in this keenly competitive field. Agents also should be well organized and detail oriented, as well as have a good memory for names and faces and business details, such as taxes, zoning regulations, and local land-use laws.

The beginner usually learns the practical aspects of the job under the direction of an experienced agent. This includes focusing on the use of computers to locate or list available properties or identify sources of financing.

Many firms offer formal training programs for both beginners and experienced agents. Larger firms generally offer more extensive programs than smaller firms. More than a thousand universities, colleges, and junior colleges also offer courses in real estate. At some institutions, a student can earn an associate's or bachelor's degree with a major in real estate; several offer advanced degrees.

Many local real estate boards that are members of the National Association of Realtors sponsor courses covering the fundamentals and legal aspects of the field. Advanced courses in appraisal, mortgage financing, property development and management, and other subjects also are available through various National Association of Realtors affiliates.

Compensation for Real Estate Sales

Commissions on sales are the main source of earnings for real estate agents and brokers. Few receive a salary. The rate of commission varies according to the type of property and its value. The percentage paid on the sale of farm and commercial properties or unimproved land usually is higher than that paid for selling a home.

Commissions may be divided among several agents and brokers. The broker and the agent in the firm that obtained the listing generally share their part of the commission when the property is sold; the broker and the agent in the firm that made the sale also generally share their part of the commission.

An agent's share varies greatly from one firm to another. The agent who both lists and sells the property maximizes his or her commission.

Real estate agents and brokers who usually work full-time have median yearly earnings of about $31,500, but earnings could be a low as $10,000 or less or exceed $75,000.

A beginner's earnings often are irregular because a few weeks or even months may go by without a sale. Although some brokers allow an agent a drawing account against future earnings, this practice is not usual with new employees. The beginner, therefore, should have enough money to live on for about six months, or until commissions increase.

The Downsides

In addition to lean income periods, sometimes a deal can fall through at the last minute. For example, buyers might get prequalified for a mortgage, based on their income and amount of debt, if any, and other factors. But another financial examination is conducted just before closing. If the buyers have purchased new furniture, for example, or in some other way changed their financial picture, it can kill the deal.

Agents also have to be very careful when dealing with new clients who are strangers. This is especially true for women realtors. Brokers will encourage their agents to work in pairs if possible and to always arrange the first meeting with the client to take place at the office, not at the property. Another precaution is not to take anybody in your car but have clients follow you in their own cars.

There are many times when you show a client twenty properties and you don't sell a thing. You can spend a lot of time, but most agents don't look at it as wasted time. It gives you a chance to increase your knowledge of different properties new to the market. You can always use that information for the next call.

Travel Sales

Out of all the industries worldwide, travel and tourism continue to grow at an astounding rate. In fact, according to the Travel Works for America Council, it is the second largest employer in the United States (the first being health services). Nearly everyone tries to take at least one vacation every year, and many people travel frequently on business. Some travel for education or for that special honeymoon or anniversary trip.

Constantly changing airfares and schedules, a proliferation of vacation packages, and business/pleasure trip combinations make travel planning frustrating and time consuming. Many travelers, therefore, turn to travel agents, who can make the best possible travel arrangements for them.

Depending on the needs of the client, travel agents give advice on destinations; make arrangements for transportation, hotel accommodations, car rentals, tours, and recreation; or plan the right vacation package or business/pleasure trip combination.

They may also provide information on weather conditions, restaurants, and tourist attractions and recreation. For international travel, agents also provide information on customs regulations, required papers (passports, visas, and certificates of vaccination), and currency exchange rates.

Travel agents must learn about all the different destinations, modes of transportation, hotels, resorts and cruises, then work to match their customers' needs with the services travel providers offer.

Travel agents generally work in an office and deal with customers in person or over the phone. But first of all, they listen to the needs of their customers, then try to develop the best package for each person. They may work with a variety of clients—affluent, sophisticated travelers, or first-timers such as students trying to save money and travel on a budget. They could book a simple, round-trip air ticket for a person traveling alone or handle arrangements for hundreds of people traveling to attend a convention or conference.

Some travel agents are generalists; they handle any or all situations. Others specialize in a particular area, such as cruise ships or corporate travel. Travel agents gather information from different sources. They use computer databases, attend trade shows, and read trade magazines. They also visit resorts or locations to get firsthand knowledge about a destination.

They have to keep up with rapidly changing fares and rates, and they have to know which carriers offer the best packages and service. Their most important concern is the satisfaction of their clients.

Since travel providers understand that travel agents are more likely to sell what they have enjoyed, most travel agents are offered free trips to help familiarize them with a particular cruise line, safari adventure, exclusive resort, or ecological tour. Travel agents also receive discounted travel on other business trips as well as on their own vacations.

Travel agents often base recommendations on their own travel experiences or those of colleagues or clients. Travel agents may visit hotels, resorts, and restaurants to judge, firsthand, their comfort, cleanliness, and quality of food and service.

The Downsides

Many travel agents relate that one downside of this career is that they don't have enough free time to do all of the traveling that they would like to do. They are often tied to their desks, especially during peak travel periods such as the summer or important busy holidays. A newcomer would get to take at least one week of vacation a year, more once they've gained some seniority.

The work can also be frustrating at times. Customers might not always know what they want, or their plans can change, and, as a result, the travel agent might have to cancel or reroute destinations that had already been set. There are times when things go wrong, such as a snow-in at an airport and people miss their connections, or someone in the family becomes ill and they have to cancel their whole cruise reservation at the last minute.

Qualifications and Training for Travel Agents

Formal or specialized training is becoming increasingly important for travel agents since few agencies are willing to train people on the job. Many vocational schools offer three- to twelve- week full-time programs as well as evening and Saturday programs. Travel courses are also offered in public education programs and in community and four-year colleges. A few colleges offer bachelor's and master's degrees in travel and tourism. Although few college courses relate directly to the travel industry, a college education is sometimes desired by employers. Courses in computer science, geography, foreign languages, and history are most useful. Courses in accounting and business management also are important, especially for those who expect to manage or start their own travel agencies. Several home-study courses provide a basic understanding of the travel industry.

The American Society of Travel Agents (ASTA) and the Institute of Certified Travel Agents offer travel correspondence courses. Some travel agencies also provide on-the-job training for their employees. A significant part of this focuses on computer instruction. These computer skills are required by employers to operate airline reservation systems.

Experienced travel agents can take an advanced course, leading to the designation of Certified Travel Counselor, offered by the Institute of Certified Travel Agents. The institute awards a certificate to those completing an eighteen-month part-time course. It also offers certification, called Designation of Competence, in North American, Western European, Caribbean, or South Pacific tours.

Travel experience is an asset since personal knowledge about a city or foreign country often helps to influence clients' travel plans. Experience as an airline reservation agent also is a good background for a travel agent. Travel agents need good selling skills. They must be pleasant and patient and able to gain the confidence of clients.

Beginners often start working side-by-side with someone more experienced in the agency. They might be placed in a specific department, for example, handling European travel, cruises, car rentals, or airfares. Much of their time will be spent coordinating and arranging details.

Travel agents must also compete with all the other travel agents in the field and need to know how to promote their services. This may be accomplished by presenting slides or movies to social and special-interest groups, arranging advertising displays, and suggesting company-sponsored trips to business managers.

Those who start their own agencies generally have experience in an established agency. They must generally gain formal supplier or corporation approval before they can receive commissions. Suppliers or corporations are organizations of airlines, cruise lines, or rail lines. The Airlines Reporting Corporation, for example, is the approving body for airlines. To gain approval, an agency must be in operation, be financially sound, and employ at least one experienced manager/travel agent.

Compensation for Travel Sales

Experience, sales ability, and the size and location of the agency determine the salary of a travel agent. Depending on the agency, you could start out earning an hourly wage or a yearly salary. Some travel agents prefer to work on a commission basis. That way, the more trips they sell, the more money they earn. A salary plus commission provides the best compensation combination.

Travel agents who are good salespeople can also earn bonuses or more free or discounted trips. If your pay is initially low, it can be offset by this added benefit.

According to a Louis Harris survey, conducted for *Travel Weekly* magazine, annual earnings for travel agents are as follows:

- less than one year of experience—$16,400

- from one to three years—$20,400

- from three to five years—$22,300

- from five to ten years—$26,300

- more than ten years—$32,600

Salaried agents usually have standard benefits, such as insurance coverage and paid vacations. Self-employed agents must provide these for themselves.

Earnings of travel agents who own their agencies depend mainly on commissions from airlines and other carriers, cruise lines, tour operators, and lodging places. Commissions for domestic travel arrangements, cruises, hotels, sight-seeing tours, and car rentals are about 10 percent of the total sale; and for international travel, about 11 percent. Agents may also charge clients a service fee for the time and expense involved in planning a trip.

Words from the Pros

Introducing Marty Gorelick, Sales Professional

Marty Gorelick has a bachelor of arts degree from LIU in Brooklyn, New York, and eight years of experience in computer hardware sales. He has also attended seminars from all of the major computer manufacturers: Compaq, IBM, Hewlett Packard, Sony, Apple, and NEC. He is account manager for county government sales at GE Capital IT Solutions in Miami, Florida, where he services Metro-Dade, Broward, and Pasco Counties, plus all cities, towns, and villages within these municipalities.

"The computer industry is constantly changing," he says. "It is the fastest-growing industry in the world. Computers have made communications possible at lightning speed.

"Scientists, doctors, engineers, lawyers, manufacturers, teachers, those in the arts, and every other element of our society operates at higher levels of proficiency than ever before because of computers. For example, a doctor in Seattle can supervise a surgical procedure in an operating room located in Atlanta through the aid of a computer hookup. Ten short years ago, this was impossible. Using a process called computer-aided design (CAD), engineers can design structures that will withstand stress far beyond their intended safety limits. Police can track known law offenders well outside of their jurisdictions and notify other law enforcement officers of potential problems. This, by far, is only the tip of the iceberg. Computer applications are endless.

"A typical day for me begins when I arrive at my office about 6:30 A.M. After running the branch's allocation reports for all the salespeople in our office, I check my voice mail for any emergency issues that must be addressed quickly. An example might be a critical shipment that hasn't arrived on time or a file server that has developed a problem and is inoperable. These situations demand my immediate attention. If both these situations exist, I'll contact our Atlanta facility to run a tracer and our service department to check out the server on the first call of the day.

"I read my E-mail messages next. It's not unusual to have between five and fifteen messages ranging from company updates to manufacturer price changes to additions and deletions from any number of vendors. Since I give my E-mail address to my customers, I might see a request for a quotation on a product or a clarification of a service agreement or a question about the configuration of a particular computer setup. Some messages require a response ASAP; others can be addressed during the course of my regular business day.

"Next stop is my in box, which usually contains a collection of faxes that have arrived since I left the office at the end of business yesterday. These faxes could contain purchase orders, manufacturer promotional notices, seminar information, or news of a prospective customer looking for a great reseller like ours! All this, and the clock has not yet struck 8 A.M.

"Now, the doors swing open and my fellow employees arrive. The phones go off night ring and our customers start calling in. We field calls concerning products, service, availability, additions, deletions, and changes in orders.

"During the course of the day, the staff may all meet for a quick meeting to discuss a change in plans concerning a new company procedure. Our regularly scheduled sales meeting takes place at 8:30 A.M. sharp each Wednesday. This is when we discuss our progress as a group and host manufacturers who are introducing new products.

"We constantly update our price list to remain the most competitive reseller in the marketplace. I do a special electronic price list for the county every sixty days. This process usually takes me anywhere from three to four working days. I also provide a manuscript of five thousand plus items from a third party vendor. On any given day, I may accompany a manufacturer downtown to the county building, where we will call on a number of departments that have requested information or a demonstration of a new item.

"Afternoons are generally reserved for cleaning up all unfinished projects, faxing quotes, looking for odd items that appear on purchase orders, and filing away purchase orders and invoices. My day ends about the time that local traffic starts to build on the highway. This represents a ten-plus-hour day, five days a week, four-point-three weeks a month. To say this is a hectic day is putting it mildly. However, if you enjoy what you do, it can be and *is* a labor of love.

"The most enjoyable part of my position is helping my customers understand their needs in respect to the use of the equipment. An example would be a customer interested in a laptop computer to do presentations at remote sites versus a client needing a laptop for communicating to his home base.

"If I had to pick a project I least like to perform, it's the tons of paper work that is a necessary evil in the day-to-day flow of business.

"The upside of my business is the satisfaction of being productive and helping others do the same. When I complete a project with confidence in a timely manner so my customers can enjoy productivity, I take a moment to sit back and breathe easy.

"The downside is always the fact of being in a race with the clock. I try never to let the clock win. I also refuse to let a discontinued product stop me from saying to a customer that I can't fill their needs. Somewhere out there is a replacement part. All salespeople are part detective. We look until we find what we need to help our customers.

"For those who are considering entering my world, I would say to be prepared to plan for a very exciting career. Technology advances as fast as you can absorb yesterday's breakthroughs. Pick a school that offers the career path that you wish to follow (sales and marketing, computer network engineering, or service and repair). Attend as many seminars in the field as possible. Read as many journals that pertain to your area of interest. Spend as much time as you can afford talking to those around you in that particular field. Don't be afraid to roll up your sleeves and get your hands dirty. Ask a million questions. Experiment with the knowledge you've gained. Share your findings with others and always remember that, to achieve success, you must make learning a lifelong endeavor."

Introducing Donna Maas, Business Owner and Sales Professional

Donna Maas' formal studies include interior architecture, design, drafting, and oil painting. With a background in graphic art, she designs all marketing materials and packaging for MAAS Polishing Systemes of Willowbrook, Illinois. She serves as president and CEO of the company.

After six years of using various cleaning and polishing products and always wishing for something better, Maas asked a chemist to assist her in formulating a product that worked. The end result is MAAS Polishing Creme, a product that quickly restores all metals, fiberglass, Plexiglas and dull oxidized paint work to an unusually brilliant finish. "Little did I realize how this innovative formula would revolutionize the polishing products industry," she says.

"The job is glamorous, hectic, and unpredictable," Maas explains. "My role encompasses product development, designing marketing materials, and fielding calls from major retailers while maintaining balance in the offices, warehouse, and factory. This, combined with extensive traveling and television appearances on QVC to demonstrate my products, requires tremendous stamina. Everyone within the company, from my executive assistant to the shipping department, will tell you that every project I tackle must be treated with urgency, requiring immediate attention. This keeps my office personnel (including myself) operating at an unusually fast pace.

"By the third year in business, I experienced an 800 percent growth on my initial investment," she says. "It is tremendously fulfilling to obtain such rapid success and worldwide recognition. I would have to think long and hard if asked what the downside of my career is because I can't think of anything!

"I would advise others who wish to get into this field to stay focused. The most difficult thing for an entrepreneur to do is to focus. You have so many things coming at you all at once. I have learned to concentrate on the most promising opportunities. When you become scattered and attempt to address every opportunity, your success is hindered."

Introducing Jim LeClair, Sales Owner and Business Professional

Jim LeClair is the owner and sales manager for Advanced Computer Services, Inc., in Lawrence, Kansas. He earned a high school diploma and took some secondary accounting and business classes. He also has engaged in ongoing seminars and classes that are offered by suppliers to enhance sales, technical training, and product knowledge.

"I was burned out on retail and on working for others," he says, "so my wife and I decided to form our own business. She had a strong computer background and I had more of the business background. We felt our strengths would complement one another. Our company consists of training and network installations, network design to integration, support, and fiber optics, to name a few.

"We have five employees. Our store hours are Monday through Friday from 8 A.M. until 5 P.M. The atmosphere is as relaxed as possible, business casual Monday through Thursday, casual on Fridays. Our busiest time of the year is summer.

"I try to keep politics out of the workplace and am flexible with my employees and their families as much as possible. Overtime, for instance, is kept to a minimum.

"A day can change within the first five minutes you walk in the door. You have to be able to juggle things around to grease the squeakiest wheel. I generally arrive at 7 A.M. and leave between 6:30 and 7 P.M., spending approximately 30 percent of my time administering to the customers' needs, 40 percent working on sales, and 30 percent on the day-to-day activities of running the business.

"What I like best is seeing how happy the customer is when we say, 'This is how the network will work,' and then the network performs as well or better than we anticipated. What I like least is having to discipline employees or contemplate lost sales.

"To be successful in this kind of work, it's very important to keep abreast of the current technology at all times, to be a good listener, to be flexible, to be able to read people, and to understand what they really want, not what they say they want. You have to be able to think quickly on your feet and have a semi-aggressive nature. You just can't take 'no' for an answer. Still, you must sell the customers what they want. Don't try to sell people something that isn't right for them just because you can make some money.

"I'd advise those who are considering computer sales to be honest, to be fair, and *always* to do a good job. Our business has grown because we have gained the trust of both our customers and our employees."

For More Information

By contacting the following professional associations, you can obtain more information about each category of sales.

Retail Sales

Information on careers in retail sales may be obtained from the personnel offices of local stores, from state merchants' associations, or from local unions of the United Food and Commercial Workers International Union.

General information about retailing is available from:

National Retail Federation
701 Pennsylvania Avenue NW
Washington, DC 20004-2608

Services Sales

For details about employment opportunities for services sales representatives, contact employers who sell services in your area.

For information on careers and scholarships in hotel management and sales contact:

The American Hotel and Motel Association (AH&MA)
Information Center
1201 New York Avenue NW
Washington, DC 20005-3931

Manufacturers' and Wholesale Sales

Information on manufacturers' agents is available from:

Sales and Marketing Management International
Statler Office Tower
Cleveland, OH 44115

Insurance Sales

General occupational information about insurance agents and brokers is available from the home office of many life and casualty insurance companies. Information on state licensing requirements may be obtained from the department of insurance at any state capital.

Information about a career as a life insurance agent also is available from:

National Association of Life Underwriters
1922 F Street NW
Washington, DC 20006

For information about insurance sales careers in independent agencies and brokerages, contact:

National Association of Professional Insurance Agents
400 North Washington Street
Alexandria, VA 22314

For information about professional designation programs, contact:

American Society of CLU and ChFC
270 Bryn Mawr Avenue
Bryn Mawr, PA 19010-2195

Society of Certified Insurance Counselors
3630 North Hills Drive
Austin, TX 78731

Society of Chartered Property and Casualty Underwriters
Kahler Hall
720 Providence Road
P.O. Box 3009
Malvern, PA 19355-0709

Real Estate Sales

Details on licensing requirements for real estate agents, brokers, and appraisers are available from most local real estate and appraiser organizations or from the state real estate commission or board.

For more information about opportunities in real estate work, contact:

National Association of Realtors
777 Fourteenth Street NW
Washington, DC 20005

Information on careers and licensing and certification requirements in real estate appraising is available from:

American Society of Appraisers
P.O. Box 17265
Washington, DC 20041

Appraisal Institute
875 North Michigan Avenue, Suite 2400
Chicago, IL 60611-1980

Travel Sales

Information on sales careers in the travel industry can be obtained from:

American Society of Travel Agents
1101 King Street
Alexandria, VA 22314

Association of Retail Travel Agents
1745 Jefferson Davis Highway, Suite 300
Arlington, VA 22202

Institute of Certified Travel Agents
148 Linden Street
P.O. Box 56
Wellesley, MA 02181

CHAPTER FIVE

Careers in Politics

When a man assumes a public trust, he should consider himself as public property. THOMAS JEFFERSON

A re you drawn to important issues that face the country and our world? Do you aspire to serve your fellow men and women in a very special way? Do you enjoy the idea of being in the center of the public eye? Then consider following a path to a political career.

Zeroing in on What Political Professionals Do

At the top of the political hierarchy are public office holders, including mayors, governors, supervisors, senators, representatives, and, of course, the president and vice president of the country. All of these individuals are elected to administer government. They handle all of the business of a city, town, state, county, or the country as a whole. It is their job to pass laws to keep order, to set up special programs to benefit people, and to spend the taxpayers' money on goods and services. As problem solvers, they meet with community leaders to find out the needs of the people and then search for ways to meet those needs.

There are many other levels of political careers. This would include those who work for political change in their neighborhoods both as citizen activists and in an official capacity—such

95

as precinct captain. Some of these jobs are voluntary, unpaid positions that could eventually lead to paying positions. Most positions, except appointed government managers, are elected by their constituents. Nonelected managers are hired by a local government council or commission.

Chief Executives and Legislators

Government chief executives, like their counterparts in the private sector, have overall responsibility for the performance of their organizations. Working in conjunction with legislators, they set goals and then organize programs to attain them. They appoint department heads who oversee the work of the civil servants who carry out programs and enforce laws enacted by their legislative bodies. They oversee budgets specifying how government resources will be used, and they ensure that resources are used properly and programs are carried out as planned.

Routinely, chief executives meet with legislators and constituents to discuss proposed programs and determine their level of support. They frequently confer with leaders of other governments to solve mutual problems. Sometimes, in the case of the U.S. president, they have to make painful and difficult decisions, such as breaking diplomatic relationships with other countries or even declaring war.

Chief executives nominate citizens to boards and commissions, solicit bids from and select contractors to do work for the government, encourage business investment and economic development in their jurisdictions, and seek federal or state funds. Chief executives of large jurisdictions rely on a staff of aides and assistants, but those in small jurisdictions often must do much of the work themselves.

Legislators are the elected officials who pass or amend laws. They include United States senators and representatives, state senators and representatives, county legislators, and city and town council members.

Legislators may introduce bills in the legislative body and examine and vote on bills introduced by other legislators. National legislators make decisions on issues such as the types of weapons the country will need for defense, how much money should be spent on the space program, and how to protect the environment. In preparing legislation, they read staff reports and may work with constituents, representatives of interest groups, members of boards and commissions, the chief executive and department heads, and others with an interest in the legislation. They generally must approve budgets and the appointments of department heads and commission members submitted by the chief executive. In some jurisdictions, the legislative body appoints a city, town, or county manager. Many legislators, especially at the state and federal levels, have a staff to perform research, prepare legislation, and help resolve constituents' problems.

Both chief executives and legislators perform many ceremonial duties such as opening new buildings, making proclamations, welcoming visitors, and leading celebrations. It is both a privilege and an important responsibility to serve in public office.

Working Conditions for Political Professionals

The working conditions of chief executives and legislators vary with the size and budget of the governmental unit. Time spent at work ranges from meeting once a month for a local council member to sixty or more hours per week for a United States senator.

United States senators and representatives, governors and lieutenant governors, and chief executives and legislators in large local jurisdictions usually work full-time year-round, as do county and city managers. Many state legislators work full-time while legislatures are in session (usually for two to six months a year) and part-time the rest of the year. Local elected officials in many jurisdictions work a schedule that is officially designated part-time but actually is the equivalent of a full-time schedule when unpaid duties are taken into account.

In addition to their regular schedules, chief executives are on call at all hours to handle emergencies.

Some jobs require occasional out-of-town travel, but others involve long periods away from home to attend sessions of the legislature. Opportunities for political jobs may be found throughout the country.

Qualifications and Training Required for Political Professionals

Voters seek to elect the individual they believe to be most qualified from among a number of candidates who meet the minimum age, residency, and citizenship requirements. There are no formal educational requirements for public office holders. However, successful candidates must be able to show the people that they are qualified for the jobs they seek, and a good education is one of the best qualifications a candidate can offer.

Successful candidates usually have a strong record of accomplishment in paid and unpaid work in their districts. Some have business, teaching, or legal experience, but others come from a wide variety of occupations. In addition, many have experience as members of boards or commissions. Some candidates become well known for their work with charities, political action groups, political campaigns, or with religious, fraternal, and social organizations.

Management-level work experience and public service help develop the planning, organizing, negotiating, motivating, fundraising, budgeting, public speaking, and problem-solving skills needed to run an effective political campaign. Candidates must make decisions quickly, sometimes on the basis of limited or contradictory information. They must inspire and motivate their constituents and their staffs. They need to appear sincere and candid and be able to present their views thoughtfully and convincingly. Additionally, they must know how to hammer out compromises and satisfy the demands of constituents. National and statewide campaigns require massive amounts of energy and stamina, as well as superior fund-raising skills.

Town, city, and county managers are generally hired by a council or commission. Managers come from a variety of educational backgrounds. A master's degree in public administration, including courses such as public financial management and legal issues in public administration, is widely recommended. Virtually all town, city, and county managers have bachelor's degrees, and the majority hold master's degrees. Working in management support positions in government is a prime source of the experience and personal contacts required in eventually securing a manager position.

Generally, a town, city, or county manager in a smaller jurisdiction is required to have expertise in a wide variety of areas. Those who work for larger jurisdictions specialize in financial, administrative, and personnel matters. For all managers, communication skills and the ability to get along with others are essential.

Advancement opportunities for elected public officials are not clearly defined. Because elected positions normally require a period of residency, and local public support is critical, officials can usually advance to other offices only in the jurisdictions where they live. For example, council members may run for mayor or for a position in the state government, and state legislators may run for governor or for Congress. Many officials are not overly politically ambitious, however, and do not seek advancement. Others lose their bids for reelection or voluntarily leave the occupation. A lifetime career as a government chief executive or legislator is rare except for those who reach the national level.

Town, city, and county managers have a better-defined career path. They generally obtain master's degrees in public administration then gain experience as management analysts or assistants in government departments working for committees, councils, or chief executives. They learn about planning, budgeting, civil engineering, and other aspects of running a government. With sufficient experience, they may be hired to manage a small government and often move on to manage progressively larger governments over time.

Compensation for Political Professionals

Earnings of public administrators vary widely, depending on the size of the government unit and on whether the job is part-time, full-time and year-round, or full-time for only a few months a year. Salaries range from little or nothing for a small town council member to $200,000 a year for the president of the United States.

According to the International City/County Management Association, the average annual salary of chief elected county officials is about $25,600, while chief elected city officials is about $12,200. ICMA data indicate that the average salary for city managers is about $70,600, while that of county managers is about $86,700.

According to the National Conference of State Legislatures, the salary for legislators in the forty states that paid an annual salary range from about $10,000 to $47,000 per year. In six states, legislators received a daily salary plus an allowance for expenses while legislatures were in session. Two states paid no expenses and only nominal daily salaries, while two states paid no salary at all but did pay a daily expense allowance. Salaries and expense allowances are generally higher in the larger states.

Data from *Book of the States, 1996–97,* indicate that gubernatorial annual salaries ranged from $60,000 in Arkansas to $130,000 in New York. In addition to a salary, most governors received perquisites such as transportation and an official residence.

In 1997, U.S. senators and representatives earned $133,600, the Senate and House majority and minority leaders $148,400, and the vice president $171,500.

Words from the Pros

Introducing Vera Marie Badertscher, Campaign Manager and Consultant

Vera Marie Badertscher earned a bachelor of arts degree and a bachelor of science degree in education from Ohio State University in 1960. Her major was theater and English. She went on to secure a master's in fine arts from Arizona State University in 1976, focusing on theater.

"Originally I served as campaign manager for many years," Badertscher says. "More recently I have been employed as a campaign consultant.

"I started as a citizen volunteer in city projects," she explains. "As a young mother, I wanted a better library system in Scottsdale, Arizona, where I lived, so I volunteered for a committee. There I met office holders, was invited to serve on their advisory committees, and eventually asked and received pay for managing a city council election campaign.

"I enjoyed the sense of accomplishment of working in politics—of being able to promote my beliefs and make things happen," she says. "I also enjoyed the fact that most people involved in politics are action oriented, optimistic, true believers. My chief asset was an ability to figure out the best way to communicate political messages and move people to action.

"My volunteer work in a federated woman's club gave me experience in bringing diverse people together to work on projects, combining government and private energies, communications, and organization of projects. My theater background helped me focus on short-term, collaborative projects.

"As a campaign manager, I spent most of my time communicating with volunteers—mostly on the phone but sometimes in memos or in newsletters. It is a very intense job because of the limited time for a political campaign (usually about nine months—perhaps symbolic?). Someone advised me, when I managed my first Congressional campaign, that during the last couple of weeks of the campaign, I would be making a dozen decisions every hour, and one in twenty or so would be truly important.

"Prioritizing is critical in political campaigns," she stresses. "You need to know the difference between decisions that do not affect the outcome (what color the signs are) and decisions that do (whether the candidate should attend a particular debate).

"A campaign manager rounds up diverse interest groups, volunteers, the candidate and his or her family, advertising personnel, researchers, and fund-raisers. The key to being successful is keeping the focus on what will get the candidate elected and not allowing anyone in the campaign to draw the focus in another direction. You can expect to talk on the phone all day, check off on other people's work, and stay close to the candidate to keep him or her on track. Generally you are trying to keep the budget down, so the work surroundings are on the primitive side—borrowed furniture and unpainted walls. You can count on noise and constant activity. (If it's quiet, you're probably losing.) This presents a hard atmosphere to concentrate in, but that's the job.

"A campaign consultant has more luxury of time to think than does a campaign manager. The consultant typically analyzes voting data history; studies the candidate, the opponent, and the voters; and writes a strategic plan for bringing the voters to support that candidate. Some consultants specialize in media or mail, but I have been a generalist, doing strategy and writing direct mail materials. The consultant works in an office or home office and meets weekly or biweekly with the candidate, the campaign manager, and others involved in the campaign. Once the plan is written, the consultant is available to help fine-tune the plan, make adjustments, review media plans, determine what to ask in polling, and interpret the results. While the campaign manager's job is not done until the polls close on election day, the consultant's job is done a few days prior to the election when no more mail can be sent or advertising launched that will affect the outcome.

"I most like the ability to work out the puzzles involved in bringing together the circumstances, the candidate, and the voters in order to persuade them that they will be better off electing that candidate. I like the thinking and the communicating of politics.

"What I least like is having to be nice to a bunch of people I might not particularly like or admire. However, I have been fortunate in being able to choose the candidates I work for, so I have worked for people I believe in and personally support. However, politics is about coalition building, so sometimes the expression 'politics makes strange bedfellows' is all too true.

"I am frustrated with the general disdain for politics and the growing cynicism, which I fear will damage our democracy," she says. "So, I would like to be able to persuade people that there are good and worthy people in elected office. My hat is truly off to the people who do participate—by voting or by running for office or by supporting those who run.

"I would advise anyone interested in entering this kind of work to introduce yourself to a candidate you admire and volunteer to help. Political science classes teach theory, but only campaigning teaches campaigning. Don't try to tell the candidate how to run his or her campaign or volunteer to be the brains behind the organization until you have actually done some of the grunt work of campaigning and learned it from the inside out. You'd be surprised how many people come to a campaign manager and say, 'I'm really good at strategy,' when all the campaign manager really needs is someone to go out in a pickup truck and put up signs. And before doing any of that—register to vote. Read up on the issues. And last, but not least—VOTE."

Introducing Wade Hyde, Political Consultant

Wade Hyde earned a bachelor of arts degree in education and history from East Texas State University in Commerce, Texas. He continued his education and received a master of arts degree in urban affairs from the University of Texas at Arlington. He also earned a master of arts degree in civic affairs teaching from the University of Dallas in Irving, Texas. He has served as a campaign manager volunteer consultant, as a civic volunteer board member, and as a planning and zoning commission member in Irving, Texas, for four years. Currently he serves as a member of the regional transportation board and a member and officer of the Visiting Nurses Association.

"In 1980, I began volunteering in organizations supporting interests with legislative agendas," he says. "Political events were at the center of what I found to be most interesting and exciting in earlier years. These events included listening to the presidential nominating conventions (before pollsters and analysts took all the fun and suspense out of final outcomes) on the radio and waiting in the town square for the results of local elections on hot June Saturday nights. History studies and government were naturally interesting and easy for me. No other subject particularly intrigued me. Politics and policy is my calling.

"Attending the unique program at the university, now called the Institute of Culture and Humanities, cofounded by Dr. James Hillman, was an eye- and mind-opening experience. The course of study encouraged use of the imagination and the heart.

"Political consulting is seasonal work, and the season can last for three months to two years, depending on the type of campaign—local, regional, or national," Hyde explains. "Political campaigning at a local level is extremely concentrated, normally three months, entered into by a candidate who has sometimes given very little serious thought about preparation of voter lists, coalition building, fund-raising, or issue presentation. The nature of the political candidate is usually one of tremendous energy and strong ego with an unshakable belief that the voting populace cannot live without his or her leadership. The consultant, on the other hand, must bring some order and a consistent, coherent message to the candidate and the workers. The atmosphere is one of chaotic, pressure-cooker days and nights.

"Everything is always late, unexpected, and includes last-minute and last second decision making—sometimes like flipping a coin and forging ahead or backtracking. The days start as if the nights had never quit, and each workday lasts about eighteen hours. Both the candidate and campaign workers contract battle fatigue, which doesn't end until weeks after election day. Saturdays and Sundays are not exempt.

"Each new campaign and candidate comes with the promise of a better day and a better way. It's exciting and hopeful to be involved in making a positive change by helping elect someone who can make a big difference. At least that's the upside. The downside is the exhaustion and condensed pressure of a compact campaign effort, and, if such should occur, the loss of the candidate's best effort.

"I would advise others interested in entering this field to understand fully and honestly why you are working for a candidate. Know if you're primarily in it for a job, an appointment, for the experience and excitement, or for the candidate. Be realistic and don't hang around too long because burnout can set in quite soon. See *Wag the Dog* and *Primary Colors*—I found them to be pretty accurate as campaign compilations."

Introducing K. Mark Takai, Elected State Representative

K. Mark Takai earned a bachelor of arts degree in political science in 1990 and a master of public health degree in health education in 1993 from the University of Hawaii at Manoa, Honolulu. During his internship for his master of public health degree, he worked for a city council member for the City and County of Honolulu.

"My experiences at the University of Hawaii as an undergraduate student, graduate student, and employee probably attracted me to the state capitol," he says. "It was through these years that I had the most interaction with the legislators. I now serve as an elected state representative, representing District 34, part of Aiea and part of Pearl City (both located near Pearl Harbor on Oahu).

"The job of an elected official interested me from when I was a young child (probably from fourth grade, when I was involved in student government). I continued to be involved with student government in high school, serving as the student body president for a 2,400-student school and in college as the student body president, representing more than 12,000 students. I truly enjoy all opportunities to interact with people from diverse backgrounds and interests.

"I declared my candidacy for public office in July 1994, won the primary election in September, and was declared the winner of the seat after the general election in November.

"The job of a state representative runs the gamut. There are probably three different 'jobs' of an elected official—very diverse, but all very important.

"The first is my job as a community leader. This is probably the most rewarding part of being in public office. The interaction with the community—through the schools, community organizations, neighborhood board meetings, etc.—provides me with the opportunity to listen and then respond to the desires and concerns of the public.

"This part of the job can also be very difficult. In the more than four years since first being elected, I have been very fortunate in that I have not had too many difficult meetings with the public; however, as a freeway project is currently being planned and the project calls for possible public condemnation of private property, I have had my fair share of angry constituents. Most times, though, I am able to work with the residents of our community to address their concerns.

"The second part of my job is as a lawmaker. Constitutionally, this is my most important responsibility. Seventy-five legislators decide what laws are passed.

"My third responsibility is as a politician (i.e., a political candidate). State house offices are up every two years, so since my first election in 1994, I have had to run two reelection campaigns. This is a very time-consuming process. The campaign season begins around July of even-numbered years and doesn't end until the general election in early November. Aside from raising money to run a successful campaign (marketing materials, brochures, advertisements, etc.), the most difficult and time-consuming tasks of the political season are sign waving (waving to cars along the roadside in the mornings and afternoons) and door-to-door canvassing.

"A typical day for me depends on the time of year. During the legislative session (January to May), a typical day begins at 7:30 A.M. with a breakfast. Then it's off to the state capitol for committee meetings, which begin at 8:30 or 9 A.M. We have private meetings in our offices or we catch up on phone calls before the House floor session at noon. Then it's time to eat lunch with constituents or go to a luncheon after the session. At 2 P.M. we start our committee hearings, which usually run until 7 P.M. After the committee hearings, I usually participate in community meetings, which usually run to 10 P.M.

"I usually keep Friday evenings free from office work and routinely spend that time with my wife. Saturdays are generally busy with committee hearings or community events. Sundays are typically days reserved for family activities.

"During the off-election year, nonsession months, I usually work in the office planning for upcoming events. As the state cochairman of Hawaii's Children and Youth (in October) for the past three years and as the state cochairman of Hawaii's Junior Miss Scholarship Program (in January) for the past two years, I find myself sometimes even busier than during the legislative session.

"The period of nonsession months during the campaign season is really tough and grueling. And, including time spent at receptions, dinners, etc., I probably spend about seventy hours a week working. However, the people I work with, both in the state capitol and throughout the community, make my job most rewarding. I would not trade the experiences that I have had for any other job. Although it can be very stressful and time consuming, I truly enjoy my job as a state representative.

"I derive great pleasure from doing for others. For instance, one of my most rewarding moments occurred when I was able to provide assistance in getting funds to build a new traffic signal at an intersection that saw many near accidents, numerous accidents, and one fatality.

"The least enjoyable part of my job is knowing full well that every bill that we pass and that becomes law has a negative impact on someone or on a specific profession. Although I have voted for many bills that do much good for our community overall, sometimes it is these same bills that get people laid off from their jobs, etc. Knowing this causes me great pain.

"I would encourage anyone interested in pursuing this kind of career to talk to people about what their concerns are. Meet with various community leaders in your community. Get involved with political campaigns and/or volunteer or work for an elected official. And if you are truly serious, begin your plans for an eventual run for public office. Good luck!"

For More Information

Information on appointed officials in local government can be obtained from:

International City/County Management Association
777 North Capitol Street NE, Suite 500
Washington, DC 20002

Democratic National Committee
Young Democrats of America
430 South Capitol Street SE
Washington, DC 20003

Republication National Committee
310 First Street SE
Washington, DC 20003

The Congressional Management Foundation
513 Capitol Court NE, Suite 100
Washington, DC 20002

CHAPTER SIX

Careers in Marketing and Advertising

We grew up founding our dreams on the infinite promise of American advertising. I still believe that one can learn to play the piano by mail and that mud will give you a perfect complexion. ZELDA FITZGERALD

HELP WANTED: MARKETING PROJECT DEVELOPER. The headquarters of a nonprofit corporation engaged in providing occupational skills and educational opportunities to employees of a large manufacturing facility seeks a qualified individual to take on a variety of administrative and educational projects. The position requires a high degree of initiative, excellent problem solving, communication, and writing skills. The successful applicant will have a college degree, perhaps a master's degree in marketing, project management, or a related field, and working knowledge of MS Office Suite 97. Competitive salary commensurate with experience. Excellent benefits provided.

Is the above ad of interest to you? Would you enjoy helping companies determine what the needs and desires of the public really are? If so, consider a career in marketing or advertising.

Zeroing in on What Marketing Professionals Do

Well before the sales team hits the road with its merchandise or services, another team of professionals—product developers, and marketing, advertising, public relations, and publicity experts—must perform its duties first. The goal of marketing is to reach the consumer—to motivate or persuade a potential buyer; to sell a product, service, idea, or cause; to gain political support; or to influence public opinion.

The fundamental objective of any firm is to market its products or services profitably. To do so, an overall marketing policy must be established, including product development, market research, market strategies, sales approaches, advertising outlets, promotion possibilities, and effective pricing and packaging.

Marketing executives determine the demand for products and services offered by the firm and its competitors and identify potential consumers such as business firms, wholesalers, retailers, government, or the general public. Mass markets are further categorized according to various factors such as region, age, income, and lifestyle.

In small firms, all marketing responsibilities may be assumed by the owner or chief executive officer. In large firms, which may offer numerous products and services nationally or even worldwide, experienced professionals working together coordinate these and related activities.

The Role of the Marketer

In simple terms, salespeople try to encourage people to buy what they are selling and marketers try to figure out what consumers have a need for. Marketers start at the beginning of the cycle and look at the customer asking themselves, "I wonder what they need." Once that is determined, marketers look at their company and ask themselves, "Do we know how to produce it and can we make money doing it?"

The Steps Involved

Once marketers come up with a product idea—the ideas might come from talking to customers or be generated in brainstorming sessions—they start communicating with the product development department, which in some industries might consist of scientists or engineers. They form a team that includes marketing management, marketing researchers, engineers, advertisers, a financial advisor, and eventually salespeople.

First the team must decide if the product idea is something the customers really want. This process involves doing market research. Market researchers set up focus groups, bringing a group of customers together and talking to them, finding out what isn't working in their present environment and what they truly need.

Professionals working in market research departments are tuned in to the consumer—what he or she worries about, desires, thinks, believes, and holds dear. Market researchers conduct surveys or one-on-one interviews, utilize existing research, test consumer reactions to new products or advertising copy, track sales figures and buying trends, and become overall experts on consumer behavior.

Agency research departments can design questionnaires or other methods of studying groups of people, implement the surveys, and interpret the results. Sometimes research departments hire an outside market research firm to take over some of the workload. For example, a market researcher could come up with a procedure to test the public's reaction to a television commercial; the outside firm would put the procedure into action.

Marketing research assistants report directly to a research executive and are responsible for compiling and interpreting data and monitoring the progress of research projects.

After the market research is conducted, marketers attempt to quantify that need in the marketplace. If thirty people have told them they need a particular device, that suggests a strong need, but the company can't afford to build something for just thirty people. It wants to make sure there are enough people out there who are willing to buy the product. This sparks another round of research.

With successful research results, the concept development stage begins. This is the development of a word or paragraph that describes the product. In some instances, marketers then take that to engineers who develop a prototype.

The prototype is taken to the marketplace for testing and evaluations. With feedback in hand, the team begins to make product improvements.

Once the company is at least 95 percent sure this is the product they want, they give it a final test in the marketplace. They also test for claims. For example, a company might want to claim that its new hospital bed will prevent skin sores, but it needs to be able to document that claim.

If all test results point to being able to move forward, the engineers start figuring out how to mass produce the product and marketers plan how the company can make money on it. For that, they have to look at the production cost and how much customers would be willing to pay for it. One of the big misconceptions in this area is that you take the cost and add a profit percentage to it. Prices are not determined that way. They are determined by what people are willing to pay.

The next step is promotion planning. Now that the company has a product, it has to find a way to get the word out. The appropriate team members make brochures and design advertising. At the same time, the numbers are being crunched and production schedules are set up. Marketing experts need to know how fast the product can be made, how quickly it can get out to the field, how many will be bought, and how big the profit will be.

Once a date is set for introducing the product, the sales force is brought in and taught how to present it. Then the product is monitored to see if it's meeting its sale projections. If it's not making the projected numbers, top management wants to know why and what is going to be done about it. Often, though, if it is making the numbers or doing better, top management still wants to know why. That's the way it goes in a competitive business.

Where the Jobs Are

Marketing professionals are found in virtually every industry, including motor vehicle dealers, printing and publishing firms, department stores, computer and data processing services firms, management and public relations firms, and advertising agencies.

Because marketers and advertising professionals work hand in hand, many marketing departments are located within corporate advertising departments or within private advertising agencies. Private marketing firms function similarly to advertising agencies and work toward the same goals—identifying and targeting specific audiences that will be receptive to specific products, services, or ideas.

Experts advise that you start your job search before you near graduation. Those who arrange internships for themselves have an edge; they've already become familiar faces on the job. When an opening comes up, a known commodity, someone who performed well during the internship, is going to be chosen over an unknown one.

Learn as much as you can about the agency or firm you're interested in. In other words, target your prospects.

Working Conditions

Marketers work long hours, often including evenings and weekends. Working under pressure is unavoidable as schedules change, problems arise, and deadlines and goals must be met.

Marketing managers meet frequently with other managers; some meet with the public and government officials. Substantial travel may be involved. For example, attendance at meetings sponsored by associations or industries is often mandatory.

The Downsides

Although marketing is considered by many to be a step up from sales, there's a downside to it. If the company is not making the expected profit, marketers could easily lose their jobs. Their responsibilities for sales volume and profit are the same that salespeople must meet.

In essence, marketers make an agreement with sales departments and personnel. For example, they think, 'OK, we are going to sell a hundred units of X product to a particular customer.' But if they spend too much money in product development or advertising and then sell only ninety units, though the salesperson has the first responsibility, the marketing people are also responsible. They had agreed on what could be sold on specific advertising and on setting a certain price. If the mark is missed, it's the marketers' jobs that are also on the line.

Another downside is that marketers usually supervise salespeople, but the sales force often makes more money than the marketers do—possibly a lot more money. But to make up for it, marketers usually also receive a good pension plan and bonuses.

Qualifications and Training for Marketing Professionals

Several educational backgrounds are suitable for entry into marketing jobs, but many employers prefer a broad liberal arts background. A bachelor's degree in sociology, psychology, literature, or philosophy, among other subjects, is acceptable. However, requirements vary depending upon the particular job.

Most marketing positions are filled by promoting experienced sales and technical personnel, such as sales representatives, purchasing agents, buyers, product or brand specialists, advertising specialists, promotion specialists, and public relations specialists.

The best marketers have a dual background, including sales experience and a formal education, ideally an M.B.A. Some start off in sales first, then after they've been on the job for a while, they go back to school for their master's, before moving into marketing.

For marketing management positions, some employers prefer a bachelor's or master's degree in business administration with an emphasis on marketing. Courses in business law, economics, accounting, finance, mathematics, and statistics are also recommended.

In highly technical industries, such as computer and electronics manufacturing, a bachelor's degree in engineering or science combined with a master's degree in business administration may be preferred.

Familiarity with computerized word processing and database applications is also important for all marketing positions.

People interested in becoming marketing managers should be mature, creative, highly motivated, resistant to stress, and flexible yet decisive. The ability to communicate persuasively, both orally and in writing, with other managers, staff, and the public is vital. Marketing managers also need tact, good judgment, and exceptional ability to establish and maintain effective personal relationships with supervisory and professional staff members and client firms.

Getting Ahead

Because of the importance and high visibility of their jobs, marketing personnel often are prime candidates for advancement. Well-trained, experienced, successful managers may be promoted to higher positions in their own or other firms. Some become top executives.

Managers with extensive experience and sufficient capital may open their own businesses.

In small firms, where the number of positions is limited, advancement to a management position may come slowly. In large firms, promotion may occur more quickly.

Although experience, ability, and leadership are emphasized for promotion, advancement may be accelerated by participation in management training programs conducted by many large firms. Many firms also provide their employees with continuing education opportunities, either in-house or at local colleges and universities, and encourage employee participation in seminars and conferences, often provided by professional societies.

Numerous marketing and related associations sponsor national or local management training programs, often in collaboration with colleges and universities. Courses include brand and product management, international marketing, sales management evaluation, telemarketing and direct sales, promotion, marketing communication, market research, organizational communication, and data processing systems procedures and management. Many firms pay all or part of the cost for those who successfully complete courses.

Some associations offer certification programs for marketing managers. This is a plus because certification is a sign of competence and achievement in this field.

While relatively few marketing managers currently are certified, the number of managers who seek certification is expected to grow. For example, Sales and Marketing Executives International offers a management certification program based on education and job performance. The American Marketing Association is developing a similar certification program for marketing managers.

Compensation for Marketing Professionals

According to the most recent National Association of Colleges and Employers survey, starting salaries for marketing majors average about $29,000. The median annual salary of marketing managers was $46,000 in 1996. The lowest 10 percent earned $23,000 or less, while the top 10 percent earned $97,000 or more. Many earn bonuses equal to 10 percent or more of their salaries.

Surveys show that salary levels vary substantially, depending upon the level of managerial responsibility, length of service, education, and the employer's size, location, and industry. For example, manufacturing firms generally pay marketing managers higher salaries than nonmanufacturing firms.

According to a recent survey by *Advertising Age* magazine, the average annual salary of a vice president in marketing is $133,000. Other surveys show a range from $25,000 to $250,000 for marketing managers, depending on the level of education, experience, industry, and the number of employees he or she supervises.

Zeroing in on What Advertising Professionals Do

"The breakfast of champions." "Where's the beef?" "When it rains, it pours." Such phrases are familiar to most of us because of the effective work that advertising specialists have been performing for years. Some consider this phenomenon a nuisance that interrupts television programming and encourages people to buy products that may or may not be the best for them. Others look upon it as a great public service. A dominating force in our society, mass-media advertising is a multimillion-dollar industry dating back to the invention of movable type in the mid-1400s.

Advertising Agencies

Virtually every type of business makes use of advertising in some form, often through the services of an advertising agency. The American Association of Advertising Agencies defines an advertising agency as "a service company that earns its income from planning, creating, producing and placing printed advertisements and broadcast commercials for its clients." Agencies may also offer additional services, such as market research, sales promotion, television programming, and public relations.

Agencies that are diversified and handle many kinds of advertising are called full-service advertising agencies. Other, more specialized agencies, may handle only one area, such as direct marketing.

An advertising agency may consist of only one employee or perhaps several thousand. Salaries will tend to be higher for those employed at bigger full-service agencies, because plum accounts like IBM or Pepsi Cola are more likely to engage larger advertising agencies.

Many people think the world of advertising is glamorous and exciting—and certain aspects can be. However, as Karen Cole Winters explains in *Your Career in Advertising*, "If you go into advertising expecting a constant whirl of fun and excitement, you'll probably be disappointed."

Agency Staff

The work at each agency is frequently divided among several individuals or departments—usually including the following:

- *Account executives* make sure that clients' work is completed satisfactorily and on time. Account executives must be savvy about their agencies and aware of each client's desires and needs. Their responsibilities lie more in the business arena than in the creative aspects of the business.

- *Art directors* must be able to effectively present a theme or idea in convincing visual form through illustration, color, photography, or cinematography.

- *Creative directors* supervise all employees and oversee all activities in the agency. At the top of the hierarchy, creative directors must, of course, be creative and possess people skills and solid business acuity.

- *Researchers* seek to determine what kind of audience would be interested in a particular product or service, why they are interested in the product, and how the public is reacting to advertising campaigns already in place.

- *Media people* work in the department that ensures that commercials are aired on radio and television and that ads get into magazines and newspapers.

Other advertising positions include television producers, print production managers, graphic artists, illustrators, photographers, freelance writers, print production personnel, and traffic managers.

Advertising Copywriters

Advertising copywriters are the real creative force behind advertising campaigns. They are the ones who dream up the words for commercials and advertisements and conjure up the themes for advertising campaigns. Copywriters may also be responsible for creating articles about products or services, sales promotion materials, public relations items, billboards, and promotional brochures.

Copywriters usually begin their work by meeting with the client and or/ account executive. After gathering as much information as possible, they let their imaginations flow while looking for a slant on why a product or service is different from all others of its kind. Then they proceed to launch a new advertising campaign with their innovative ideas.

Qualifications and Training for Advertising Specialists

Most employers expect applicants for advertising positions to have college degrees. For those who aspire to become account executives, an M.B.A. is especially important. Many schools offer programs in advertising, and a number of top advertising agencies offer in-house training programs for copywriters and account managers.

Since copywriters deal with a wide cross section of ideas and concepts, a general liberal arts background in combination with business is particularly valued. Courses in such subjects as economics, history, journalism, marketing, advertising, math, social sciences, speech, literature, business administration, human relations, and creative writing are recommended.

Copywriters need the skills that all writers should have—the ability to produce clear, concise prose. Therefore, gaining writing experience—in the form of published articles; participation in school, church, or yearbook publications; or internships with local newspapers or radio or television studios—is worthwhile.

Candidates should prepare a portfolio containing at least three ads from two or three previous advertising campaigns. These can be class assignments or real ads from actual clients. If you have no advertising experience at all, present potential employers with samples of your published writing.

Compensation for Advertising Specialists

There is a considerable range of salaries in this field, particularly in different regions of the country. The median annual salary in advertising agencies is about $35,000. Junior copywriters may start out with as little as $15,000; writers with senior status may earn $50,000 to $100,000 and even more as creative directors.

The larger the agency or account, the higher the salary will be. The best locations for jobs are in large cities such as New York, Chicago, Detroit, Boston, Atlanta, Dallas, Minneapolis, and Los Angeles.

Words from the Pros

Introducing Edward Pitkoff, Marketing and Advertising Professional

Edward Pitkoff, of Omaha, Nebraska, attended the Philadelphia Museum School of Art, the Pennsylvania Academy of Fine Arts, Temple University, and Studio School of Art and Design, all in Philadelphia. He also attended a wide variety of marketing and advertising seminars and the School of Visual Arts in New York for a course in television production and direction. He has held several high-ranking positions in marketing, advertising, and sales and is founder and president of Creative Decisions, Inc., of New York.

"My career began in 1961," says Pitkoff. "After twelve years in positions of designer, assistant art director, art director, and creative director, a freelance business presented itself and I formed Ed Pitkoff Studios, which expanded and evolved into Creative Decisions, Inc., in 1973, and there the story truly started.

"The idea of doing high-quality creative advertising that could convince a consumer to purchase a product was very attractive to me. Early on, one thing that had a profound effect on me was having a mentor who taught me how to marry the communication to the consumer so that the buyer could visualize themselves as part of the product.

"Don't ever become distracted," says Pitkoff. "Always keep your focus on the business of advertising. And remember, what *you* might want to say to sell this product or service really isn't important. The only thing that *is* important is what would be compelling to the consumers. What do they want to hear? What do they want to buy? Ultimately, it is the consumers who judge how well your message has come across. If the product sells, then you know your focused communication has reached its audience."

Introducing Dennis Abelson, Marketing and Advertising Professional

Dennis Abelson earned a bachelor of arts degree in classical languages from Washington University in St. Louis, Missouri, and subsequently earned a master of science in journalism degree in advertising from Northwestern Medill School of Communications in Evanston, Illinois. He has experience as a copywriter, associate creative director, and creative director.

"Ten years ago I was making a substantial living as a freelance writer," he says. "But the isolation and lack of significant, bigger-budget creative challenges was starting to bring me down. Then I was contacted by Don Tomala, my future partner, who had come across one of my promotional mailings. He was in the process of establishing an integrated, full-service marketing consulting and communications firm to fill a gap he had experienced as a Fortune 500 sales and marketing director. After a somewhat rocky start (it was the middle of an economic recession and few companies had even heard of integrated marketing), we eventually bootstrapped ourselves into a successful, growing company. Two years ago, Tomala and I disassociated ourselves from a third partner and changed our corporate name from the Figa Group to Matrix Partners.

"Our current client roster comprises a highly eclectic mix of companies that turn to us for a wide range of services, including packaging, advertising, promotions, direct mail, and sales presentations. In 1997 we became agency of record for Anixter International, a global distributor of computer cabling and networking systems. We also serve the Quaker Oats Continental Coffee Division, the American National Can Flexible Packaging Group, Vitner's Potato Chips, the Dive Equipment and Marketing Association, and MS BioScience, a fast-growing agricultural biotech company.

"I originally got into the creative end of advertising because I couldn't see myself holding down a nine-to-five job. It also gave

me the opportunity to keep pursuing my interests in audio engineering and cartooning. In my undergraduate years, I was program director of the campus radio station as well as the creator
of a weekly comic strip in the campus paper.

"There is no typical day in this industry, which is why it
attracts so many people. But it might unfold somewhat like this:

- 8:00 to 9:00 A.M.—Revise ad copy, circulate for internal
  review.

- 9:00 to 10:00 A.M.—Project status meetings—logistics, costs
  to date.

- 10:00 to 10:30 A.M.—Finalize ad copy, fax to client.

- 10:30 to 11:00 A.M.—Review logo designs and alternate
  color treatments for new brand.

- 11:00 to noon—Perform on-line trademark search for
  proposed theme line.

- noon to 1:00 P.M.—Lunch at desk while drafting new
  business presentation.

- 1:00 to 1:30 P.M.—Client call regarding new promotion.

- 1:30 to 4:00 P.M.—Conceptualize with designer and writer
  on direct mail project.

- 4:00 to 4:30 P.M.—Internal meting—refine thinking on new
  business presentation.

- 4:30 to 5:00 P.M.—Edit PC-based presentation for biotech
  client.

- 5:00 to 6:00 P.M.—Finalize new business presentation.

- 6:00 to 7:00 P.M.—Continue conceptualizing on direct mail
  project, take home to finish up.

- 9:00 to 11:00 P.M.—Finish writing direct mailer.

"What does it mean to be doing my kind of work?" asks Abelson. "At times it seems totally thankless, but in what other profession do you get paid to legally hallucinate, to play creatively with concepts and pictures?

"Here is my list of upsides:

- No time for corporate politics or hidden agendas.

- The opportunity to be knowledgeable with more than a hundred different industries.

- The satisfaction of contributing visibly and dramatically to the success of a client's business.

"And here are the downsides:

- The hours.

- Certain clients who shall remain nameless.

- Certain clients who play it safe when they should be competing.

- Logistical and budgetary constraints on creativity.

"I would tell others who are considering a career in advertising and marketing to start with the largest organization that will hire you. And be prepared for the long haul."

Introducing Jane Ward, Marketing Professional

Jane Ward received a bachelor of arts degree from Catholic University in Washington, D.C. She majored in English, with minors in French and philosophy, and subsequently earned a master of philosophy degree (Irish literature major) from Trinity College in Dublin, Ireland.

"I came back to the United States from Ireland in 1995," she says, "and had a difficult time finding a job. I found that a master's degree in Irish literature is actually a handicap in the job market, particularly if you don't have much work experience. So I learned Web publishing—HTML conversion, layout, etc., and found a well-paying job that utilized these skills. Unfortunately, I found this work very boring and was only biding my time until I could get a more interesting job. In the meantime, I was promoted twice at the Web publishing job, proving to potential employers that I could manage well in a professional environment.

"When a job as a marketing specialist came up at a software company, it was a perfect fit. I had proven that I could learn technical aspects of a job, and I was able to provide my employers with some writing samples. So since 1997, I have been creating public relations and marketing materials for that software company. I now hold the position of senior marketing specialist.

"I write website content and manage the site by supervising the graphic designers and approving graphics to go on the Web. I am in charge of press releases and ad copy, and I supervise the production of the ads. I also go to about six or seven trade shows per year, staffing the booth or speaking to the press about our company. I also help out with product documentation by editing it for style and grammar, though I don't do technical writing, per se.

"I work about fifty hours each week. And since I recently switched from a PC to a laptop, I have been able to bring work home with me. This is both good and bad, I've found. It provides convenience but sometimes I feel as if work has invaded my home life too much.

"I'm very busy, but the work environment is pretty relaxed with a very deliberate casualness. In software, people often wear very casual clothes and look down on typical corporate types who wear suits and work in the big city. Also, software, as an industry, is still very young. This is evidenced by the fact that the average age of people working for my company is probably less than thirty years.

"I enjoy writing something, a press release for example, and then seeing that it was picked up and published by a magazine. It gives me a thrill to see such immediate results of my work. But I don't like going to trade shows because I don't enjoy traveling and having to spend time away from my family. Also, they can get pretty tedious. However, I do understand that it's important for our company to be seen at important shows.

"To individuals who are considering this type of career—I would say learn how to start looking at the world around you with a critical eye. When an ad comes on television, pay attention to it. What was the goal of the people who created it? Who is their target market? What elements did they pull together to create the ad?

"Since I am involved in the writing end of marketing, I would recommend that you learn how to write truly well. I've seen so many college graduates—even those of Ivy League schools—who can't write a complete sentence. And I strongly recommend a liberal arts education, which teaches you how to think and how to articulate your thoughts. These are the kinds of tools that you need to achieve success in any industry."

For More Information

The following professional associations can aid in your job search. Many of the publications these organizations produce are available in public libraries.

The American Marketing Association is a professional society of marketing and market research executives, sales and promotion managers, advertising specialists, academics, and others interested in marketing. It fosters research; sponsors seminars, conferences, and student marketing clubs; and provides a place-ment service. It also offers a certification program for marketing managers. The organization publishes the *Journal of Marketing*, *Journal of Marketing Research*, *Journal of Health Care Market-ing*, and an international membership directory. For more infor-mation, write to:

American Marketing Association
250 South Wacker Drive
Chicago, IL 60606

Members in the National Council for Marketing and Public Relations are communications specialists working within com-munity colleges in areas including alumni, community, gov-ernment, media, and public relations as well as marketing, publications, and special events. The association works to foster improved relations between two-year colleges and their commu-nities. The association holds an annual conference with exhibits, national surveys, and needs assessments and publishes a journal called *COUNSEL*. Additional information can be obtained by contacting:

National Council for Marketing and Public Relations
364 North Wyndham Avenue
Greeley, CO 80634

Sales and Marketing Executives International offers a man-agement certification program. Write to:

Sales and Marketing Executives International
458 Statler Office Tower
Cleveland, OH 44115

CHAPTER SEVEN

Careers in Public Relations and Fund-Raising

Publicity is the life of this culture—in so far as without publicity capitalism could not survive—and at the same time publicity is its dream. JOHN BERGER

HELP WANTED: MANAGER OF COMMUNICATIONS AND PUBLIC RELATIONS. You will manage internal and external communications and public relations activities and implement special events and projects. You will also work with media and vendors, maintain a presence on the Internet, measure effectiveness of programs, and direct the writing of press releases, brochures, public service announcements, newsletters, and flyers. At least five to eight years of experience in public relations and communications is required, along with strong interpersonal and analytical skills and proven writing abilities. Bachelor's degree in communications, journalism, or public relations required. Experience in a health care environment is preferred. We offer competitive wages and a strong benefits package. Forward your resume with salary history to us immediately.

Does this want ad inspire any career interest? Many extroverts feel that their calling is to work in the fields of public relations or fund-raising.

Zeroing in on What Public Relations Professionals Do

You might be surprised to learn that the concept of public relations is definitely not a new invention. It dates back to 1787, during the time of the Constitutional Convention. And in the 1800s, both the North and the South made use of the media during the Civil War in an attempt to persuade the populace to adopt their way of thinking.

The goal of public relations remains the same—to sway the public in a particular direction, or to build, maintain, and promote positive relationships between two factions: the agencies (or companies) and the public.

Public relations professionals may be self-employed or hired by public relations companies. They may also find work in the PR departments of a variety of concerns, such as political parties, nonprofit organizations, hospitals, colleges and universities, trade unions, financial institutions, social service organizations, or clothing companies.

Business and industry rely on corporate public relations to educate the public about their products and services. And since nonprofit organizations do not generally advertise, they count on public service announcements provided by public relations professionals to get their messages out.

Public Relations Work

The work of a public relations practitioner falls into six main categories:

1. *Research.* This includes all of the preliminary work that is undertaken to ascertain the client's goals so that a plan to achieve them can be devised. Library research, client interviews, surveys, opinion polls, and collecting data are all part of this.

2. *Program work*. Once research is completed, a plan is set up based upon the findings.

3. *Writing and editing*. This may come in the form of press releases, presentations to clients, internal memos, reports, and magazine articles.

4. *Special events*. Included in this category are press conferences, special appearances, and autograph signings. All are carefully orchestrated to gain the greatest amount of attention.

5. *Media placement*. It is important to select the most important information to release, choose a good time to release it, and send it to the most advantageous receivers.

6. *Fund-raising*. Fund-raising is what sustains nonprofit organizations. Possible events include membership drives, direct solicitation, and benefit banquets.

Those who work as generalists in the field must be able to perform a wide array of duties at the same time. On any given week they may write press releases for one client, design a brochure for another, approach an editor for a third, meet with a talk show host for a fourth, implement a promotion for a fifth, set up a press conference for a sixth, put together a press kit for a seventh, work out the beginnings of a client contact for an eighth, and field media questions for a ninth!

In the governmental arena, public relations specialists may be called press secretaries, communications specialists, or information officers. A senator's press secretary informs the elected official's constituents of his or her accomplishments and responds to questions from the media and the press. The press secretary schedules and appears at press conferences and issues statements from his or her superior.

Qualifications and Training for Public Relations Professionals

Although there is no defined training program for public relations specialists, it is wise to combine a bachelor's degree with some public relations experience, particularly in the form of internships. Professionals in this field often have college majors in journalism, advertising, public relations, or communications. Some companies express a preference for someone with an M.B.A.

Typical courses include: public relations principles and techniques; public relations management and administration, including organizational development; writing, emphasizing news releases, proposals, annual reports, scripts, speeches, and related items; visual communications, including desktop publishing and computer graphics; and research, emphasizing social science research and survey design and implementation.

Compensation for Public Relations Professionals

Median yearly earnings for full-time public relations specialists average about $32,000. A recent College Placement Council salary survey found that new college graduates entering the public relations field were offered an average beginning salary of $21,000. According to a recent salary survey by the *Public Relations Journal,* public relations managers averaged $44,000.

In the federal government, individuals with bachelor's degrees start at about $23,000; those with master's degrees begin at $28,000. Those in managerial positions average about $46,000. A press secretary's salary generally falls between $20,000 and $70,000.

Words from the Pros

Introducing Tracy Larrua, Senior Account Executive

Tracy Larrua is a senior account executive for Macy & Associates, a public relations firm based in Venice, California. Larrua attended a performing arts high school, then entered business college but ended up working at an advertising agency instead of getting her degree. She quickly worked her way up the ladder in advertising after six years with a company called Ogilvie and Mather. She then began doing public relations work, which she has continued for the past twelve years.

"My typical day is spent writing pitch letters, developing story ideas for editors, and adding, deleting, and updating our media database to be as up-to-date as possible as to what is going on with our clients," says Larrua. "While wearing a headset, I also make a lot of phone calls. The atmosphere is never relaxed. Actually, it is usually very high stress, but it's a fun stress. Our typical work week is forty plus hours, but depending on client demand, workload, and editorial deadlines, it can easily turn into a sixty-plus week.

"Our company has the coolest environment," she says happily. "We operate from an old two-story brick firehouse that contains off-white walls with no offices but separate working areas. My space is a room with a view and two big windows that let in fresh air. The space is definitely very interactive. We have no doors. There are high ceilings and a very artsy conference room and lots of natural light. Whenever clients or friends come by, they tell us our offices look like high-tech office space. We also play music all day, and it's probably the most enjoyable and productive office environment I've ever had the pleasure of working in.

"The people I work with are great. Each of us brings different strengths to the group, and our personalities complement one another. That's key when you work in a smaller office environment. The only downside is that our company specializes in public relations for real estate and architectural clients. I enjoy this, but I'd like to bring in more consumer-type clients in the future, such as restaurants, hotels, and travel accounts.

"I would recommend that others who are interested in entering this profession get in on the ground floor and act like a sponge. Soak up everything you can," she stresses. "As you start developing your skills, you'll find yourself ascending. Also, stay flexible. This industry has gone through all sorts of changes. Learn, adapt, and adopt a fearless attitude."

Larrua also adds a word of caution. "If you aren't the 'people type,' don't even consider getting into this business. You have to be comfortable and persuasive in talking to people—all kinds of people. Remember, your personality skills count for a lot in this industry."

Introducing Betsy Nichol, Public Relations Business Owner

Betsy Nichol heads her own public relations agency, Nichol & Company of New York. She earned a bachelor of science in journalism from Boston University and has continued to enhance her credentials through seminars and professional workshops.

"I started my career as a journalist, as many public relations experts do," Nichol says. "I was lucky enough to serve a three-month internship at Fairchild Publications and then gained a full-time position with one of their (then) daily newspapers—*Home Furnishings Daily* (now *HFN*). After three and a half years there, I was recruited by a small public relations firm. Early on in my career, someone told me I should have my own business, and at the time I thought he was crazy, but as the years went by

I realized that I'm one of those people who is better at being my own boss than working for someone else.

"I was attracted to the field because of the fast pace and the realization that no two days would be alike. I knew I would always be learning about different subjects and meeting interesting people from all types of professions.

"I also like to communicate in writing, and good writing skills are essential in the PR business. There's never a dull moment in this business, and being successful requires many of the same skills as being a journalist. It's been an exciting journey.

"Being head of a public relations firm is very hectic," Nichol stresses. "The phone is always ringing, and you never know if it's a client with a crisis, an editor on a deadline, or an employee with a question.

"The public relations business is filled with deadlines and curveballs. As the head of the agency, I spend a lot of time in meetings with clients or counseling them by phone and meeting with employees to guide their progress in achieving client objectives. Other time is spent on new business activities, keeping up with industry trends, and making internal changes accordingly. Much of my time is also spent on the endless administrative tasks involved in running a business.

"I'm continually monitoring my E-mail, talking on the phone, giving instructions to staffers, and receiving countless faxes, notes, and mailed items that require a quick response. There is never enough time in a day.

"Networking is also important for my success. I attend and speak at many meetings, workshops, breakfasts, and lunches that can produce new business, provide insight into industry trends, and form strategic alliances that enable me to serve my clients better.

"The public relations business offers endless ways to express one's creativity. It also demands that one think strategically to help clients solve their problems, which keeps me on my toes and makes every day action packed.

"In running a business of twelve people, there is also a great sense of teamwork and caring among the staffers—not a typical office environment. The interaction between us produces exciting results and great fun. The downside is that we often have to cancel evening plans and work late to meet breaking deadlines.

"My advice to others who are considering this field is to work hard and be flexible and both patient and impatient in your quest for success."

Introducing Joanne Levine, Public Relations Professional and Business Owner

"My company, Chicago area-based Lekas & Levine Public Relations, Inc., specializes in pursuing media publicity for small and mid-sized businesses. Media public relations is probably the most popular among clients but also the most stressful for the practitioner. Although I also write copy for brochures and business letters and plan some special events, 80 percent of my time is spent trying to help my clients make the news—that is, helping them to appear in newspapers, magazines, and trade publications and on radio and television. My clients recognize that media publicity is a valuable tool to increase the visibility of their products or services while enhancing their images in the eyes of potential customers, suppliers, business associates, and peers. While paid advertising 'looks like an ad,' editorial appearances add credibility and help to establish the client as an authority in his or her respective field. Whether a fledgling entrepreneur or an established pillar of the business community, there are few people who wouldn't relish the opportunity to make a favorable impression in the news.

"On the other hand, my specialty is probably the least favorite among public relations practitioners. With an ad, you know what day it will appear, what size it will be, and exactly what it will say. With an article, I hold my breath until the client and I read it in the publication. With a taped interview on radio or television, I wait to see if anything was cut or taken out of context. While my press release and phone conversation with an editor might have been chock-full of the kind of information I hope they will relay to the public, there are no guarantees such as those in advertising. I work with editors and writers who are always on deadline, always overworked, but nevertheless always looking for a good angle. For these reasons, my job can be stressful and sometimes plagued with problems that are completely out of my control.

"But when all goes well, there's nothing like it. I have seen the positive results of good, steady media campaigns time and time again. And more than once in a while, a really big media appearance can make an overnight difference in someone's business. The client is on cloud nine, his or her phones begin to ring off the hook with new business, and I am showered with praise and gratitude. I often get to know my clients well and enjoy friendly, upbeat working relationships with them. The knowledge that I am helping to make a client's business grow is very rewarding.

"Although a degree in journalism or communications is certainly desirable, in my particular case, I entered this career without any real planning. Even though I majored in English in college, I didn't really have any ambition to focus on public relations. When my children were babies, I didn't even work outside the home but joined various local community groups, such as Friends of the Parks, the PTA, and a human relations group. In the course of setting up a fund-raiser for one of the organizations, I was paired with a real-life PR pro on the publicity committee. She really gave me an education, and I became fascinated with her skills.

"At the same time, my very creative brother was writing music, forming bands, and starting wacky side businesses. One of his companies created and marketed original adult board games he designed. To test my newfound skills, each time he introduced a game, I sent out press releases to the media. The first game, Danger Island, even included me as one of the characters. When the reporters arrived, I became part of the story. We got spectacular local and national coverage.

"That first project really whet my appetite. From there, I began publicizing my husband's retail stores, more civic groups, and the like. One day, I thought about the fact that I was doing a great job and not getting paid for it. I recruited my brother's wife to help me, and we wrote a press release about two sisters-in-law who started a public relations company devoted to small businesses. We got an immediate response from the local chain of newspapers. They wrote a feature article about our company, even though we had no clients. The rest, they say, is history. From that initial article, the phone began to ring, and within a month or two, we had five clients. It's been word of mouth ever since.

"My sister-in-law stayed aboard for nine years and finally decided to go back to her first love, teaching. She always felt that even if she did a great job pitching an idea to an editor, it was always that editor who determined how well we did our job. We were always caught in the middle: if the article was great, the client thought we were, too. If the article was small, all the effort we put into the project seemed insignificant. So she decided to move on. I, on the other hand, thrive on the highs and the lows. Not knowing what the day will bring seems exciting to me. One 'yes' from an editor and I'm as happy as a clam.

"If you want a career in media publicity, I would advise you to read, read, read. Study the format of newspapers, watch the twelve, five, six and ten o'clock news. Read every magazine you can get your hands on and note how things are laid out. Reporters have certain 'beats,' and if you can zero in on what they write about, half the battle is won. Familiarizing oneself with the media is a never-ending responsibility. While there are a few good media guides that provide information, this is not a substitute for studying the style of an individual person, section, or publication. Also, as the media faces the same cutbacks and consolidations as any other industry, frequent changes in person-nel happen at a rapid pace.

"If you don't want to go through the trial and error process as much as I did, try to get an internship with a PR company. I have used graduate students from the Medill School of Journalism at Northwestern University as freelancers several times. Just remember that in order to make it in this field, you need a good imagination and the ability to find an 'angle.'

"I can't tell you how many times a client has said, 'I do a better job than anyone else in town and I truly care about my customers.' That's very nice, but it's *boring!* Find out why the client does a better job. What does he or she do differently? Is the business owner an interesting person? What are his or her hobbies? The list goes on and on. You must be able to pick someone's brain until something newsworthy pops out. Then, you must learn who might be fascinated with your information, so much so that they want to inform their readers about it or share it with their television audience.

"As I look back over the weeks, months, and years, I feel that the most rewarding part of my effort is the knowledge that I have truly made a difference in my clients' businesses and, conse-quently, in their lives. The wide diversity of my clientele makes for a job that never gets boring. And when I look ahead, more than anything else, I wonder what my next subject will be."

Zeroing in on What Fund-Raisers Do

HELP WANTED: DIRECTOR OF RESOURCE DEVELOPMENT. Seek-ing an experienced fund-raising professional with a demon-strated success with private and corporate foundations and major donor development; exceptional oral and written communica-tion; solid research, planning and grant writing skills; strong relationship-development skills; solid business, goal driven, and results orientation; dynamic personality; demonstrates initiative and a creative approach to resource development. Submit vitae, related writing sample, and salary requirements.

As this want ad illustrates, fund-raisers are directly involved in planning and organizing programs designed to raise money for colleges; hospitals; political campaigns; and educational, historical, community, religious, arts, cultural, educational, social service, health, advocacy, political, trade, scientific, and research organizations. Also included are youth leadership and other charitable causes. Sometimes referred to as philanthropy, this industry ranks as one of the ten largest in the United States.

Fund-raisers are usually asked to determine the length and scope of the campaign, slogans or other phrases associated with the effort, how funds will be solicited, and who will carry out these tasks. Then they oversee the efforts to make sure things stay on schedule and go according to plan. They will regularly assess and reassess the campaign to make sure what changes may be needed.

Using enthusiasm, energy, and competence, they combine the skills of financial management, public relations, marketing, accounting, human resources, personnel management, and media communications. Assessing the viability of charitable programs, they devise strategies for meeting goals, identify potential donors, and solicit funds efficiently and effectively. In the 1990s alone, Americans contributed more than $100 trillion to educational, health, research, arts, religious, and social welfare organizations.

Fund-raisers may be known as any of the following:

• Director of Major Donor Development

• Director of Annual Giving

• Director of Major Gifts

- Development Director
- Director of Development
- Vice President for Development
- Sponsorship Director
- Director of Resource Development
- Fund-Raising CEO
- Fund-Raising Coordinator
- Fund-Raising Researcher
- Membership Director
- Development Research Coordinator
- Fund-Raising Director of Development

Fund-raisers fall into one of three general categories. The first group consists of staff members of health centers, social service agencies, community groups, nonprofit organizations, and cultural institutions. In each case, they plan and work on all fund-raising projects. For instance, a fund-raiser who is employed by a college may write to large corporations to solicit contributions.

The second group of fund-raisers works for fund-raising consulting firms. These individuals provide advice to nonprofit organizations about the best ways to raise and manage the money they accumulate. For instance, a hospital that is interested in raising money might hire the services of a fund-raising consultant.

The third group of fund-raisers works for companies that specialize in offering fund-raising events for any organization that wishes to raise money. This, for instance, might include carnivals, concerts, and theater parties.

Fund-raisers often work in temporary locations. They constantly attend meetings, present talks, and meet with volunteers.

As the campaign progresses, tension grows and the pace becomes increasingly hectic. With the stress of meeting financial goals within a limited time period, fund-raisers often need to work long hours—perhaps seven day weeks—in order to meet the designated goals.

Qualifications and Training for Fund-Raisers

Most fund-raisers have liberal arts degrees, though the degree specialty will vary, and different organizations may require specific qualifications. If you know in advance that you wish to do fund-raising for an environmental concern, for example, then it would be best to focus on a degree in something related, such as environmental studies.

Marketing degrees are also helpful, as is practical knowledge from courses such as mathematics, economics, computers, bookkeeping, and accounting. Other suggested courses include: psychology, speech, sociology, public relations, social work, education, journalism, and business administration.

Individuals considering entering this line of work should have high communication and numerical skills and be well organized and flexible. They must also have the ability to work well with others, to work under pressure, and to meet deadlines. They must be able writers and motivators. Computer skills are necessary, as they are for almost every job these days. Sales skills are also very important. In fund-raising there are also special software programs such as donor tracking programs. Some mentioned frequently are Raiser's Edge, Fundmaster, and Donor II.

Most employers seek individuals with two to seven years of experience. Internships and volunteer opportunities are ways to get experience, and nonprofits have many more volunteer opportunities than business or government jobs. With five years of experience—paid or unpaid—you may choose to become certified by the National Society of Fund Raising Executives (NSFRE).

Compensation for Fund-Raisers

Earnings for fund-raisers range from volunteers who work for nothing to those who earn a high income, perhaps $200,000 per year. A shortage of skilled personnel in this field has prompted some fund-raising counseling firms to offer performance bonuses. Here are some average yearly salaries:

Entry-level fund-raiser director—$26,000

Senior-level director—$44,556

Average fund-raiser in Northeast—$560 weekly

Average fund-raiser in Northwest—$380 weekly

Qualified fund-raisers are in high demand. Since the federal government has cut back on spending in the area of social programs, the burden of charitable activity has been thrust upon philanthropic sources.

Words from the Pros

Introducing Thomas Campbell, Director of Development and Alumni Relations

Thomas L. Campbell earned his bachelor of science degree in business administration in 1981 and a master of science degree in physical education in 1987 from the University of Delaware. He also received a master of science degree in business administration from Wilkes University in 1990.

He is a Certified Fund Raising Executive (National Society of Fund Raising Executives) and serves as director of development and alumni relations at Allentown College of St. Francis de Sales in Center Valley, Pennsylvania.

"My career here actually began in 1988," he says. "Previously I had worked in Jacksonville, Florida, as a sales and operations manager, but my wife and I were interested in moving back north. I came to Allentown College, thinking it would serve as an excellent practice interview. To my surprise, I was offered the job! I decided to accept it and stay here for a few years. Here it is, eleven years later, and I am still here! Why? Because I love the position!

"Since I had always worked in sales, the work involved was really not that dissimilar. I found that fund-raising was just another version of sales but with a wonderful twist. The work was now impacting students' lives. I know that without the money I raise, many of our students just wouldn't be able to attend college. And since I recognize the value of a college education and the impact it can have on someone's life, I am very motivated to do this kind of work.

"There are no days that are 'typical.' The overriding object is to raise money, of course, but there are lots of steps. You just don't call someone up and expect them to give you money. It's all about relationship building, cultivating people, and identifying potential donors.

"This kind of work brings much joy and is very fulfilling. I would say that the most difficult aspect of this position is that, after eleven years, it is sometimes difficult to rise to the challenge of exceeding the previous year's performance.

"I would advise others who are interested in entering this career to first secure another type of job on the corporate side. With that kind of experience to your credit, you are a much stronger fund-raiser because you understand what executives must deal with and what they are up against."

For More Information

The following professional associations can aid in your job search. Many of the publications these organizations produce are available in public libraries.

The American Marketing Association is a professional society of marketing and market research executives, sales and promotion managers, advertising specialists, academics, and others interested in marketing. It fosters research; sponsors seminars, conferences, and student marketing clubs; and provides a placement service. It also offers a certification program for marketing managers. The organization publishes the *Journal of Marketing*, *Journal of Marketing Research*, *Journal of Health Care Marketing*, and an international membership directory. For more information, write to:

American Marketing Association
250 South Wacker Drive
Chicago, IL 60606

Members in the National Council for Marketing and Public Relations are communications specialists working within community colleges in areas including alumni, community, government, media, and public relations as well as marketing, publications, and special events. The association works to foster improved relations between two-year colleges and their communities. The association holds an annual conference with exhibits, national surveys, and needs assessments and publishes a journal called *COUNSEL*. Additional information can be obtained by contacting:

National Council for Marketing and Public Relations
364 North Wyndham Avenue
Greeley, CO 80634

Information about careers in fund-raising can be obtained by contacting:

American Association of Fund-Raising Executives
25 West Forty-third Street, Suite 1519
New York, NY 10036

Association for Healthcare Philanthropy
313 Park Avenue, Suite 400
Falls Church, VA 22046

Direct Mail Fund Raisers Association
445 West Forty-fifth Street
New York, NY 10036

National Society of Fund Raising Executives (NSFRE)
1101 King Street, Suite 700
Alexandria, VA 22314

About the Author

J an Goldberg's love for the printed page began well before her second birthday. Regular visits to the book bindery where her grandfather worked produced a magic combination of sights and smells that she carries with her to this day.

Childhood was filled with composing poems and stories, reading books, and playing library. Elementary and high school included an assortment of contributions to school newspapers. While a full-time college student, Goldberg wrote extensively as part of her job responsibilities in the College of Business Administration at Roosevelt University in Chicago. After receiving a degree in elementary education, she was able to extend her love of reading and writing to her students.

Goldberg has written extensively in the occupations area for General Learning Corporation's *Career World Magazine*, as well as for the many career publications produced by CASS Communications. She has also contributed to a number of projects for educational publishers, including Free Spirit Publishing, Capstone Publishing, Publications International, Scott Foresman, Addison-Wesley, and Camp Fire Boys and Girls.

As a feature writer, Goldberg's work has appeared in *Parenting Magazine, Today's Chicago Woman, Opportunity Magazine, Chicago Parent, Correspondent, Successful Student, Complete Woman, North Shore Magazine*, and the Pioneer Press newspapers. In all, she has published more than three hundred pieces as a full-time freelance writer.

In addition to *Careers for Extroverts and Other Gregarious Types*, she is the author of sixteen other career books published by NTC/Contemporary Publishing Group, Inc.